The Cathar Message

By

Audree de Groot

The Cathar Message

By

Audree de Groot

in cooperation with

Llyn Springard

Published by Springwood House Publishing 2014,

ISBN 978-0992925505

Dedication:

'Als Catars; Als Martyrs'

Table of Contents

1 -   Introduction

In the late 1990s while I was in a long drawn out recovery from
cancer, I was in the habit of keeping a 'Student's Notebook' beside
me – I have always written poetry, and if I woke during the night
with a 'good line' I would jot it down – otherwise I would have
forgotten it by morning.

One morning in 1999 I awoke to find eighteen pages of script on the
notebook. This writing was not poetry, nor was it in my usual
handwriting, and I found it hard to decipher, because the words were
often joined together; moreover, it sometimes seemed that the
language was stilted, as if being translated into English.

Not understanding what the script was about, I telephoned my friend:
Llyn. She came to see me at once read it all, and recognized the
contents as being from the Cathars.

These were people of whom I knew nothing and I have no idea at all
of why I was singled out to be the recipient of their words, but such
was the case. They wrote of many things, and they have since spoken
to us by means through my mediumship.

This is an experience which Llyn and I wish to share with anyone
who may be interested in the Cathars, or in their system of belief and
their moral code, for we are convinced that the 'Bons Hommes' and
the 'Bonnes Femmes' of the thirteenth century Languedoc have
much to offer to humanity today, as teachers and healers and also
simply as people of probity of life.

Their simple goodness, their honesty, and their scrupulous and
incorruptible integrity of thought, ass well as their way of living,
have a lesson for today's sadly corrupt world and its inhabitants.

Via their writings and conversations the 'Cathars' have told us that
during the intervening centuries they have realised that some of their
tenets were mistaken – and we feel that this admission is a measure
of their religious strength and rigorous intellectual honesty. Clearly,
they have changed their minds after long thought and deep

consideration, and are not too proud to tell us this.

What impresses us greatly is that the Cathars have never mentioned their martyrdom - they have only spoken of how they lived, never their martyrdom. Nor do they preach, they simply state their own beliefs, never claiming that they are the only people who are 'right' – and we know now that they worked and studied with Christians, Jews and Muslims, in the schools and universities of their time.
We have reproduced the writings that the Cathars have sent through me, while I was sleeping, and also some of the conversations which we have had with them. They have spoken through me and the questions that we have asked them have produced some very interesting answers.
The conversations have occurred in both England and in the Languedoc, it does not seem to matter where we are, our friends from those far off Cathar times are always able to find where we are.
However, when we have travelled in the Languedoc they have come to visit us each evening, to give us instructions about where to go the next day, and have always promised us tht we would have good guides. We have never been let down, either with guides living now, or guides from the 13th century and neither have we ever been told of anything that did not exist or was not of specific interest. We have learned to trust our Cathar friends absolutely, for they have never misled or disappointed us, or lied to us at any time.
We have reproduced the 'automatic writings' which they have sent on many occasions; these scripts are very different from the usual 'automatic writing' in that I, the recipient, was actually fully asleep when they were written. The writings cover a wide range of subjects which, it would seem, the Cathars are anxious to lay before the world at this time. The writings have been universally clear, concise, and informative.
Not everybody will believe the claims that we make about the experiences which we report here neither do we expect that everyone will do so: we hope is that those who have a particular

interest in the subject of the Cathars will be helped and encouraged by our story.

We also hope to underline the importance of what the 'Cathars', the 'Good Christians' (as they were often known) have to offer us today.

Our intention, in writing all this down is to honour those brave and faithful souls, whose love for humanity was great - which means that they are still concerned to help people today - and to present their message: a recent conversation with a highly regarded Cathar bishop included his opinion that "All that really matters is Love'; by which he meant love for mankind. We hope that this is clear from this book. Included are some of the poems which have been presented from time to time throughout the years.

For clarity, we have used a different type face for those scripts and poems which have come to us from the Cathars themselves. For this the type face we have used is Tahoma.

Thanks are due to Llyn, who has made written records of the many hours of the various conversations that we have also had with our Cathar friends through my mediumship.

2 -   Who We Are

Llyn was in her early fifties, Audree, in her mid sixties, when the adventure began. For us it really is an adventure full of interest and fun, as well as being a deeply spiritual experience, and now, so many years later, it remains the same and is on-going. Both of us have held responsible positions during our careers, and are well educated, intelligent women who just happen to have been 'Mediums' from birth. Thus we have always been aware of the existence of that other dimension of 'being': the life of the spirit. This is something that, because we have both known it from birth, we take very much for granted, to both of us it is perfectly normal.

We have lives to live here and now: we have jobs to do and business matters to attend to. There is thus a great and pressing need to keep our feet firmly on the ground, never to allow our imaginations to run away with us, and to test every experience sand to seek confirmation before we accept and report it, and in this we have been most meticulous.

When this experience began, we neither of us knew South West France - Audree had visited her sister, then resident in Paris, and Llyn had enjoyed a couple of family holidays in Brittany with her husband and her children, when they were young.

Neither of us had studied French history – Audree knew a little about Louis XIV, because of an interest in the history of seventeenth century England, and of course we had both heard about the battles of Agincourt, Crecy and Poitiers. We had a smattering of knowledge of the French Revolution in which King Louis XVI and his Queen, Marie-Antoinette, had been guillotined, and of Napoleon. Naturally we knew something of the events in Northern France, in the First and Second World Wars.

That was the sum of our acquaintance with the history of France. Neither of us can speak the Occitan, although I speak good 'schoolgirl' French and Llyn knows a little Spanish, having worked in Spain for a little while.

The work started when I found the first piece of 'automatic writing' on my bed that morning in 1999; since then, it has been my privilege to be the Medium for more writing and also for much spoken matter. This latter usually happens when we are at peace, in the evening, and when I am relaxed. Usually, if I'm lucky, I hear the first few words of introduction and perhaps the last few words. Sometimes I have been able to hear a little more, especially if we have been travelling by car: that seems to be a time when they are able to use me while I'm awake – perhaps because we cannot do anything else but listen as we travel! It's quite a pleasure to know what is being said.

Science is at last catching up with spiritual knowledge. Quantum physicists are beginning to recognize that we are more than the sum of our physical parts, and that we have a 'state of existence' beyond the mental structures of the brain and of the physical body. They have come to this conclusion partly because of they have discovered neutrinos – the smallest particles of atoms so far found; neutrinos can be, as one scientist expressed it 'at both ends of the universe at once'. With such a discovery, it is no great wonder that scientists are beginning to understand an existence outside of, but co-existent with, the corporeal body. They cannot yet quite bring themselves to call this a soul, or a spirit, but what else of each of us exists 'outside the body'?

Further, if an atom is divided to the last degree, the only thing remaining is light – which of course means that we are, in the end, beings of light.

This book and that which it reports may seem strange, but I would like to add a quotation from Sir William Crookes, the well known and respected scientist, which was made when he had proved, beyond any of his reasonable doubts, communication between the world of spirit and the world of those still in the flesh:

"I did not say it *could* happen. I said it *did* happen".

3 - The appearance of the first 'Automatic Writings'

Autumn 1999.

The following is the first piece of writing that I found on my bed one morning. At this time I was still in a high degree of pain; this was somewhat alleviated by painkillers, taken mostly at night. These drugs had the effect of deadening my physical senses, but often, as I drifted into sleep, I would be instructed to take up my pen. The next day – or sometimes later, if the A4 pad that I kept near me had slipped down between my bed and the wall – I never had any recollection of writing after I settled down to sleep.

At this time, too, I was prompted to write the poems which we have also woven into this book.

This poem was not contrived by me but came as a whole and spontaneously, as did the subsequent prose, which arrived after I had written the poem down down, and after I had gone to sleep:

The Cathar Message

'And we went bare foot:
we had cast our shoes,
whatever we had left
of brooch or buckle,
into our cloaks, and down the cleft
beyond the battlements.
so we went barefoot
to our funerary pile,
cloak-less, with just one garment,
for propriety; for then
we were no longer needy men
and women. We had left
all riches, and all coin,
when first we came to join
in Perfect love The Cause.
Now there was less than ever pause
to think what we might need.
our mortal bodies need no longer heed
cold rain or stony pathway.
No more was needed on that day.
no longer held in check, in single file,
one by one, barefoot we went,
singing, until our breath was spent,
the Song of Perfect Joy.'

'And when we had given our promise of love and trust, and we had shown, by our actions, that we could live by the Rule of Perfection and had shown by our words that we could preach and teach the Word of Perfection; and when, furthermore, we had shown by our acts that we had learned to heal bodies and souls then we were led into the interior. The cave was lit by soft lights, shaded candles in obscuring covers. If there was no cave, then some small and safe room, may be a barn, cow-shed, or the upper room of an inn; anywhere that could be made clean, sweet, and private. There was placed a table with a candle upon it, and a dish of bread, of salt, of water and the book of John the beloved Disciple.

And there, amongst our brothers and sisters we made our professions of Faith and loyalty.

We promised to tell no lies, but to honour the Truth; and also we promised to confide the Truth to anyone who truly wished to be enlightened. We agreed also to swear no oaths, in case we should by adhering to them or by breaking them cause death or dishonour to ourselves or to others. We further promised to heal any sick person, whosoever they might be, the best that we could; and, if we were summoned to the dying, to offer them the Consolation, should they truly desire to be Consoled.

We gave our solemn word that we would never betray anyone of the Faith. Nor would we seek to deny our own part in the Faith, so be it that we were directly required to answer.

Yet we were enjoined not wantonly to place ourselves, or our brothers and sisters in Faith, in jeopardy.

Having made our profession and sworn our Promises, we were blessed by the Bishop, or else by his legitimate representative if so be he could not himself attend.

We then took Consolamentum.

From that day on, we no more ate any tainted foods, though we made no restriction on others.
From that day on, we no more resorted to sexual deeds, with anyone else, or on our own, but kept our vile and earthly bodies as pure as their situation on earth would allow.
We were scrupulous in cleanliness, truth, and loyalty, abstinence, and obedience to the laws of the Good God.
There were no mortal men who might hold us in thrall, concerning our religious duties, for all of the one Faith were equally Perfect, save that our Bishops were more learned, and were allowed to handle monies, in order that they might purchase those goods of which we stood in need. Namely, the coarse blue cloth for our robes, and this was often both spun and woven and sewn by the women of the Faith, as were our linen small clothes. Hides were purchased if we had no herds, so that parchment could be made for our scribes to write upon, and sandals could be fashioned by those Believers who had skill to fashion them, as with all our wants: vessels for food and drink, knives, and other matters for cooking and eating and storing of food and for the medical simples which we made. Our Bishop could at his will and in his knowledge of events, purchase the service of Men-at-Arms, called Sergeants-at-Arms, if none of the Believers had arms or were willing to use them and knew how to do so. This use of the armed men was a necessity which was used only when true need arose - the murder of our Believers or Perfecti, and the need to prevent more.'

The writing continued, telling how the writer's life was lived.

'For the most part we lived by what we found by the wayside as we went from farmstead to farmstead and village to village. And those common people who were Believers were often happy to furnish us with food, wine and shelter.

And if we were asked for payment and we had no money, then we paid that with salt which we carried in tight skin bags attached to the belts at our waists. And all this salt was given to us in those places where it was found and was made usable by Believers, for they knew of its value. Likewise, they were taxed for it by their lords; but where those lords were Believers also they (the lords) remitted that tax to the people, provided that the people gave that salt, which would have been the tax to the Perfecti or their known companions.

And wine likewise was given to us, but we mixed it with water and a little honey, so that we were never troubled in our minds by the intoxication of the wine.

And so we lived simply, our living was frugal, and yet we were not in want.

And when it was time for harvest, be it of fruit, grain or grapes or olives, or any other thing, then if we were in that region, the people had the help of our hands, and of the backs of those of us who were strong.

And of those of us who could read and write and the number was many, the people had the use of those skills to help them in any way that was needful to them. As, accounting to their lord for their taxes and their doings and in the making of their wills at death, the dower of their daughters wed, and the jointures of their daughters and sons, other than the oldest son.

And in these ways we paid for our bread and were in no wise

burdensome to the People. But we aided them in sickness, bringing the skill of healing, either by simples or by the Laying on of Hands, as shown by Jesus to his Followers. '

The next extract deals with nursing the sick. We have found that there were Houses for Women, that had been set up by great ladies of the times, at Fanjeaux and other places.

'And for those who were like to be sick for a long time, they were carried to the Houses of our women Perfecti, who tended the very sick until they were made whole. And if they who were very sick could not be made whole again, but were about to die to this world then the Perfected women would send for the Bishop or for his legitimate representative in that place, and if there was no one, then they sent for any Perfected man for a man dying, and for a woman dying the Perfected women themselves, and Consolamentum was given to the dying. Who, then in grace, were no more troubled with the things of this world, but were kept clean, decent, and in comfort, eating nothing, but taking water or medicines, until their death came to them. And then were their bodies carefully and decently disposed. For we knew that the soul of the departed, free from its prison of flesh, could arise in glory to be rejoined with the good God - for we believed that every soul may rejoin the Good God, if so be it had been consoled and had then remained unpolluted by the things of this world.
And there were many places where the bodies of the dead could be laid to rest after the fashion of our Faith, for the lords in that land and often even the priests, blinked at those rites and did not pursue the Believers on that account.
But where the Roman church was strong and demanded the bodies to be buried according to their rites, we transported the

dead body with speed to another place to be buried according to the Faith saying that this one or that one had expressed their will to be buried in such or such a certain place, perhaps where he or she had been born or had family ties or some such other request that made it possible for us to keep the priests of the Roman Church at bay.'

The writing discussed what the unknown writer usually ate and wore:

'And we ate only bread and fruit, nuts, vegetables and a little fish, for those things are cleanly and not the produce of the loins of animals, whereof man is also one. And we drank wine, water, or small beer, but if it was not water, then we put water to it, mixing it to ensure that we became not intoxicated but preserved the dignity of the Faith. Nor were we then tempted by the weakness of the flesh, which overcomes the drunkard. And we were careful in washing our bodies, as well as our few garments, that we were not lousy, nor carried lice or fleas with us unknowingly.

And especially we were caring to keep clean our hands, for that we laid them on the sick. So before and after we laid hands upon the sick, we washed our hands in clean water and dried them on a little towel of linen which we carried in our scrip. And we likewise washed our hands both before and after eating or preparing food, for such was the way of Jesus and he said that it was good to be clean and that the godly would be so.

And as touching the clothes that we wore, we wore no hose but we wore sandals both in heat and in cold, for they were just as good to walk in mountains as to walk in straight and easy paths. And we wore shirts of plain coarse linen and drawers of the same. And over these we wore a tunic or robe of blue cloth such as has been heretofore described. And this had sleeves to the wrists, and was close to the neck, and came a little above the ankle and hung full so that we could stride largely.

And for the night and for the cold, we had a thick cloak, also of blue, but some in dark green or black, made as it were like a blanket, but fitted to the shoulders and with a hood. And this hood was to keep warm the head, and to shade the eyes in sun and snow, and at times when it was needful to cover the face, it served this too.

And around the middle of the robe, about the waist, we wore a girdle to keep the gown shut, and a belt to carry our knife and scrip, and any bundle or bag that we needed to carry with us: for we went on foot. Our garments were in no wise like those of the priests of Rome, but we dressed as the common people, yet we were cleaner than they, for we valued the purity of cleanliness. And we were accepted among the people as if we were of themselves. Yet when we came to the courts of lords who were Believers we dressed no differently, but were still accorded an honourable place at the lords' tables and in their halls. And as they knew that we could both read and write and make tallies – for we were numerate – they would call upon us to read whatever their chaplain or their reeve had written for them, for they knew that we would deal honestly with them and so they checked the dealings of their servants.'

The writer discussed how women lived and what work they did:

'And our Perfected women had houses where they lived together in as much harmony as women can who have belief in the same Truth and profess the same Faith. And they worked there, helping to make our garments and their own and making simples, salves, and balms, nursing the sick and attending to those poor women who, as the habit of mankind is, were with child and about to come to the labour of bringing that child to life on this earth

For at that time many women died of that labour and their children went then motherless or died in the birthing as did the mother. But the Perfected women were wise in those matters and helped many who would otherwise have perished in pain, pitiful to see, and in filth and ignorance. But while those newly become mothers stayed in that House, then the Perfected women spoke gently to them of the Faith that they professed, and many women became believers also and went about to raise their children in the knowledge given to them by those Perfected women.

And in that region also, were there women who had born many children and were tired and whose health was broken with so much labour and giving suck, who came to understand that it was not a sin to sleep aside from their husband, eschewing sexual pleasures, for this kept them free from the dread of child-bearing and was not, as was told them by the priests of Rome, sinful. So were the lives of many good poor women saved, in that they no longer had to bear the burden of child-birth; but the priests of Rome, when they questioned why no children were brought for baptism, were told that the woman was now past the years of childbearing and so they asked no more.'

How the followers of the "Cathar" decided to become further
involved with the teachings:

'Moreover, mostly the husbands of those women were not
angered by wives who no longer wished to bear children, for,
if they truly loved their woman they were in dread for their
wife, her life, each time that her time came again to labour
forth a child.

And when the children grew up to young men and young
women, then it was the place of the man, their father, to give
them land or dower them. This was a hard thing for poor folk
to bear, and the more children, the harder to provide life and
dower for them. Thus were the men-folk too, brought to see
that it was good, in time, to embrace the purity of our Belief.

And so the numbers of Believers grew and this made the
priests of Rome grind their teeth and curse our Good God and
our wisdom.

Further, the lords of lands, where there was poverty, if they
were followers of our Belief, were glad to free their people
from the taxes due to the church of Rome; for they could then
take their own portion from their people, and know that the
people had still the wherewithal to eat and drink and also lay
by stores – for the taxes for Rome were grievous both to the
lords and the peasants. Moreover, the peasants then had
cause to love their good lords and to do their bidding
cheerfully, since taxes were light and they were less poor than
they had been when paying 'Peter's Pence'.

So our belief flourished, and in the valleys and hillsides there
were joyful meetings. And when anyone fell sick, his fellows
would say "Fetch quickly the Bon Homme so that this sick one
may be cured!" And if there was no Good Man then they
would fetch a Perfected Good Woman and the sick one would

be cared for until they were whole.

And if one fell or tripped or otherwise broke a bone, as in leg, arm, or foot, or any, other than the neck, so his fellows would again call on the Good Men and the Good Women and the bone would be set and healing prospered.

And many came to love those of the Belief, for the good deeds they did and the help that they gave, and for the pure and gentle manner of their life and their piety, for they were mostly of peasant stock, or of gentle stock, with no difference made in any way between them and they were neither proud nor easily offended, as were the priests of Rome. Neither did they inflict penance but knew the simple needs and problems of the common folk and loved them. And thus they were loved in return.

And the Belief flourished, and many came to be of that Faith, for they saw the purity and chastity and goodness of the Bons Hommes and Bonnes Femmes, as against the monstrous doings of the priests of Rome and also the lewdness and lack of wisdom of the nuns of Rome. And so we flourished'

The Cathar Message
'We took the Holy Book,
We ate the simple bread,
We drank the water pure;
and there was never either
son, or willing daughter,
who was not sure that soon
Perfection would be theirs:
when it was proper time,
when all the days were right.
We had most carefully
studied and learnt the way
that honesty demands
of the most humble ones
who would be Perfected
by laying on of hands
and of the Holy Book.
We burned as candles there,
living our simple Faith,
healing with simple herbs,
burning with simple Truth –
until, in truth, we burned!'

What the "Cathar" Believed, and how they differed from the Roman Catholics.

'And the wisdom which it was given to us to know was clear, and as simple as clear. And it is thus: The Good God whose Mind formed everything that exists, consulted within the Mind of God and made the world which is this earth and then God set it amongst the stars in the sky, which is the heavens. And the Good God also made all that live on the earth and all the plants, trees and everything else that is on the earth. And the Good God made all the Angels and Archangels, to do His bidding

Then Lucifer, an angel of light, being lesser than God, challenged the Good God, saying "Am I not also a god, seeing I am made by a god?" And the Good God gave that which had been made to Lucifer, saying, "My Son, since you wish to become a god, you must take this good world that I have made and see if all the animals and all the men and the women that I have made will love you. But you must remember, O jealous one, that the souls of all men and all women are Mine by right. And you can keep only those souls who you seduce away from My Path. And all souls have the right and the way to seek redemption from the yolk which you make for their necks – as you will do, seeing that you are full of pride and envy."

And so the did the Good God order all things, that all souls who remain un-consoled and unrefined must seek at the death of the body, another, new, body, in which to dwell, so that they may, having seen their fault, seek Perfection and become rejoined once more with the Good God who made them.

But Lucifer attempts to blind the eyes of the souls of mankind with his light so that he may seduce the souls away from the love of the Good God. Then the souls must stay incarnate and they continue to do evil things and say evil words and think evil thoughts and to call down evil fates upon themselves.

So they must, when the bodies they inhabit die, seek new bodies and the cycle goes round again, as the year goes from Springtime to Winter and round again. Until in time each soul finds the truth of existence, which is this: that this incarnate life is but a treadmill, chained to the engine of Lucifer, so that then they seek to break the chains which bind them unto the dung and the dirt and seek for the Truth of the Good God whose children they rightly are. Thus it was that we were taught and thus we taught all who would hear.

 And we showed them that all flesh is corruptible but that the soul can be incorruptible if it wills to reign over the body. And when the soul reigns over the body, then it becomes king over the body and with Purity and Truth it becomes again incorruptible and can return to join again the over-soul of the Good God, its true Parent and Source.

So then we had to show them how to live in the Light of the Truth of the Good God. And to that end, we taught them that it is a purifying thing to abstain from sexual activity, since this produces more people to serve Lucifer.

And we showed how it is good to avoid the product of the sexual activity of animals – eschewing all flesh and poultry, all milk and all those things which are made from milk – for the milk is intended by nature and the Good God to feed the offspring of animals, not mankind. Further to which human women do not make of the milk of their breasts either butter or cream, nor would the people wish to eat thereof. Then why should we eat of the produce of the food of the animals? And since all flesh is corruptible, and it may only corrupt mankind to eat the flesh of animals. And so it is right and good to reject the eating of these fleshes, for then is man's flesh less corruptible.

We showed the people that they were most plentifully supplied by the Good God with fruits of the earth, of the trees and plants, water in abundance and the juice of fruits, as grapes and apples and other fruits which provide liquid. Likewise are provided for us nuts and other things, such as grains that can be cooked into bread and cakes. And with all this abundance and with fish from the rivers, lakes, and sea – which are not the product of sexual union – there is food in plenty, yes, and drink also, without killing and eating animals and birds, which practise is not only inhumane, but is the cause of more corruption of the body, and of the soul. Likewise we showed the people that to drink wine and beer without restraint makes men and women foolish and taints their souls and weakens the body, as heart and brain, which are softened and made useless by the misuse of these beverages.

And we showed them how they could, like those who were Perfected, live quiet, gentle and productive lives, free from corruption and living in the Light, not of Lucifer the god of this world, but of the Good God, whose children we all are in truth. And we showed all men and women how happy and well they could be, strong to work and happy to live. And this did we accomplish by our own example, being simply clad, eating cleanly and without excess and abstaining from sexual conjunction, but not from true love, the which is infinite and comes from the Good God, who made not only the world but also Lucifer, god of this earth-world.

So men and women could become once again incorruptible parts of the Good God at their death, not having to seek for new bodies in which their souls might dwell in order to serve Lucifer, god of this world, whose other name is Asmodeus, which is to say 'god of this world', whereas Lucifer means 'light bearer'.

And because the priests of Rome were in the toils of Lucifer, they hated us and especially they hated all who were Perfected'

And we did not believe, and we still do not believe, that god can be made by a man however often he blesses bread and wine. If he does make a god, then this must be a lesser kind of god, and as all men are sinful and none perfect, then this must be an imperfect god that an imperfect man can make. And what would you have? That a man shall place himself higher than the Good God? No! That is the work of the evil god – the god of this world whose hope is always to snare both men and women away from the truth and to imprison them in his own lies, away from the Good God.

And thus no one of us is more blessed than any other, but all can call his brethren to his table to feast together.

All who truly believe as we believe can come to Perfection. When this is so they can make their profession and take Consolamentum which is that they must be consoled by their brethren for the stains of sin on their souls, which souls are given to them by the Good God, so that they are made clean again by the recognition of their misdeeds and impure beliefs and they see that because this is grievous to them, they must be consoled and made whole again. When this is done they may go forth, strong in faith and truth, to live and work in the knowledge of the Good God, and they are aware of the snares of Asmodeus, the god of this world, and able to avoid these. Then as they strive at their work in this world, whether they be tillers of the soil, or bakers of bread, or as stewards to the lords temporal, or as lords themselves, they can teach by the words of their mouths and the examples of their lives, the

Truth of the Good God and the untruths that have been done in his name. And if it be that they do well, it may be that this is their calling in the world, and they go forth, by twos, into the highways preaching the clean truth to whoso will listen.

They keep their bodies clean and chaste, taking no flesh, nor consorting in the pleasures of the flesh, but trying to be good true men and women of God the Good and Great.

So may they show other souls how to live and so may they themselves be Perfecti. In the fire of the Peace of the Good God are they cleansed, and so the people see the light that streams from these Perfected ones and praise the Good God that they can see it'.

The Writings Continue, with a reference to the Cathars' own Writings, and what they learned from others:

'Thus it happened that for safety we wrote down all that which we had learned, putting the scrolls in safe hiding places. And we met openly in those places where the lords of the lands were our friends but where we had no highly -placed friends to protect us we had perforce to meet privately in the glades of the forest, where the trees hid us, as pillars in a great church hide those worshippers who wish to be hidden, and in caves whose presence was the knowledge of very few, and also in lonely and isolated farmsteads and barns. And as the work of the priests against us became more violent, so we met ever more secretly.

To help us in extremes of danger, those who had studied deeply were able to teach those things that they had learned, so that we could preserve our freedom. Thus we had learned so to meditate that our spirits could remove themselves from our bodies; these bodies then felt no pain, being thus unaware of its presence, and the spirits, if they were seen by others, were thought to be us, in truth and in the flesh and were pursued; but since a being of spirit cannot be grasped by the hands of man, no arrest could be made and, united once more to the bodies our spirits remained unharmed and our bodies felt no ill. And this is a great gift, and it can be attained only by long study and practise.

This gift came first from the Kabbalah, written by the Israelites even before the time of Jesus the Teacher. And be warned that this feat can only be achieved with the help of a Magus and this is a long study, and if the soul cannot reunite with the body which is its present home, then that body will die and the homeless spirit must find another, new, body. And yet even so, if the spirit is that of a truly Perfected one it will again be rejoined into the Spirit of the Good God'

Caring for the sick is discussed in more detail:

'Further we learned from scholars from afar, many new ways of healing, both by the laying on of hands, as was performed by Jesus, and by the application of balms and salves and the ingestion of simples, both liquid and in pills made by the rolling of the pounded ingredients in a little water, or honey, on a flat marble slab, making of them small globes which are easy to swallow. The women Believers gathered many herbs, which they dried; the leaves they dried and certain roots they pounded up small to make salves.

And we learned surgery, to sew up wounds and mend bones when they were broken, to save suffering, and to prevent infection.

And each Perfected one, whether man or woman, was skilled in Healing, having been taught by the wise men and women which salves or potions or pills to use and which herbs were good for certain sicknesses or bad conditions of the body. But no Perfected man ministered to any woman: for these were attended always by women of the True Belief. And this was intended to prevent any lustful thought becoming uppermost in the mind when treating the sick. And where possible Perfected men treated sick or wounded men whose sickness or wound was in the body. Yet should he be sick or wounded in a limb, then a woman Perfected might attend him.

And further we sought also to mend minds that were distempered or deranged, which we did by prayer and by divers ways.

But when there was war and there were soldiers who were wounded in fighting or by other instrument of war, then whoever was closest in space to the injured one would attend on him, whether it were man or woman, since in a war there is no time for impure thought, and only the saving of life is the mind set on'.

There continues a discussion of what non–Cathars did not know about the faith:

'There were many who did not know our True Belief and they thought that we had no true religion and that we did not follow the Master Jesus. Those people who so thought were themselves deluded. For we did follow the example and the Rule taught by the Master Jesus. We gave no thought to the goods of the world, what to eat or what to wear and we went about preaching his holy teachings, we slept on the bare earth at nightfall if we came to no place where people dwelt; and we had no thought of money but gave our time, our strength, our labour and our knowledge, out of love for the Truth.

Which Truth is that all souls of men and of women too, are the property of the Good God and will return to Good God when they have learned enough of this world and are become Perfected. And all the time that these souls dwell in the earth-life, they may perfect themselves; but always the god of this world, which is called Asmodeus or sometimes Lucifer, will try to seduce the souls away from the study of Perfection, so that he might aggrandise himself, for that envious one has still not learned that there is but one true God, who has made all and to whom all belongs.'

A discussion follows on how those who do not follow a pure life are seduced by the god of the material world, and of how that they may be helped:

'And so the evil snares of Lucifer are spread out for men's souls and women's too. And these snares are many and are made especially for each soul. For that evil one knows each soul, its weaknesses, as for drinking too much wine or for lusting after women or the love of gold or for the love of the mastery of men.

And those whose snare is wine and strong drink are made not to know that they are in the snare of the evil one until they can no longer live without strong drink. And when they have given all they have earned or inherited and have vomited forth all that they have drunken and are sick within themselves and their wealth and health gone, then only do they know who has them, nose and toe. Then, belike, they will cry to the good Angels or to the Good God. And if their prayer is heard, then one of the Perfected ones can take that drunkard under his care and little by little can wean him away from the wine jar by the use of certain wise herbs and by locking the unfortunate one into his chamber with water only to drink. And some are saved.

And those that lust after women too greatly and spend all their inheritance and their health in the pursuit of women, they too become sick in the body and the mind, and are standing in need of the help of the Perfected ones, who will, if the lecher wills it, help him to eschew his wantonness and live cleanly. And if he cannot live without any lust, then he must at least slake that lust with his own wife only and so gradually will that desire leave him, and he become whole man again.

And for those whose snare is gold, there is no easy way for the helping of them, for it cannot be right for a Perfected one to take money or goods away from a man; but it may sometimes be that much teaching and example will show the miser how he stands in vanity, and in the danger of being caught by the snare of the evil one. Then sometimes by prayer he may be brought to see that he has enough for his needs, and he may live happily, giving to charity that which is not necessary for support. bare

But the miser is a coward, for he will not leave his gold in case it may be stolen. And the lover of lechery cannot take himself away from his doxy, and the drunkard is a fool. But he who lusts for power will use all ways to find power, and all means to support it. And he will use what power he so gets, to get more.

But we are taught that no matter how far into the mire of sin and evil a soul might fall, yet, when it is reborn into a new body, it then can again begin the work of perfection. And the work of the Perfected is to lead souls to seek for perfection while they live in their their earthly body, whatever life may be like at that time,and to show and direct them into good pathways, not into the mire and ditches.

And this was and is the reason for the much learning of the Perfects, for it takes much knowledge so to deal with all souls. And all the while they are working with the people not yet perfected, the Perfected ones must be always on guard that they do not themselves fall into snares of corruption: for that is an easy path and the first steps may be delightful. But the wise know how better to deport themselves so that they take no backward step, but go forward always, bringing with them such souls as they may teach.

And in this do the Perfected ones seek to resemble the master Jesus, when he claimed for himself that he was the shepherd of the flock, meaning that he showed the way and led those who were with him and followed his advises and his ways.'

So what was the Faith for which these Good Men and Good Women, and their followers (known as 'Croyants' or Believers) were prepared to go to their deaths rather than to forswear? The answer is a simple Faith: they believed that the Good God the 'Holy Father' of their main prayer, is the Maker and Ruler of World of the Spirit, 'Heaven', the 'Summerland' 'the After-life' or whatever you care to call Perfection; and this earth is the domain of the lesser god, 'Asmodeus' or 'Satan', or simply 'darkness'. They held that Jesus, whose simple principles they followed, was not a god, but an advanced Being who carried the Christ Spirit, and they followed his injunction to love one another, to teach and to heal. .

They believed that the souls of all humanity are indeed part of God, their Holy Father, but that they must return to live in the material world on numerous incarnations, in order to experience and to learn and understand more so that they might be worthy to rejoin the Spirit of God.

Cathars did not expect the average 'believer' (croyant) to live austerely as the Perfecti, but if someone had the correct spiritual personality,was mature, and had experienced life fully then that person could be trained to be 'perfected' and could possibly also learn the esoteric arts. There were mostly simple and were very similar to mediumship and Spiritual Healing as practised by honest mediums and healers today. A de G.

The writer describes how the Cathars differ from Roman Catholic priests:

'And sadly it was not the way of the priests of the Roman Church to live like the Master they were sworn to serve; it was for this cause that our Belief was born, because of the corruption of the church of Rome, taking for the name of them that followed the clean way the Greek word 'Catharsis', namely 'Perfection', for that is what we sought and seek still. Which name was first cast at us as a sneer, but by which, for our good living, we became known.

And we seek not to fetter men by chains that bind them and by causing fear in their hearts as do the Roman priests and others we have heard of, but we seek to make people happy through their seeking after Truth, Honesty, thrift, and kindliness. And so we seek to heal, not to hurt, as do the torturers of other religious ways, and we seek to labour in the field with the harvesters of grapes and wheat, for by doing this we harvest also their souls to be saved, and so returned to the Good God who made us and them.

For we are simple men and women though we are wise, and we know that all come naked into the world and that all must go naked out of the world, and we take nothing with us but our souls when we leave this earthly life. Therefore we must seek to have as good souls as we well may, since they were lent to us by the Good God and to the Good God must they return. For if they are not good, then must they be delivered up to Asmodeus, god of this world, to live again in a human body so that he may again ensnare them and decoy them away from their true nature and home, which is with, and part of, the Good God, who made all things.

And all these things are told that it may be understood that we worked for our personal wisdom and knowledge; and not only for our own salvation but also for the aid of all others, souls who were wishful to be with the Good God and His ways, and be His servants.

 And it was in this wise that we worked at harvest and healing, and for this aim that we went forth from place to place, telling our fellow men, who are our brothers and sisters in God, how they may find the right Way and Path to the health of their immortal souls and be rejoined with the Good God.

And it was for this that we learned writing and the arts and sciences of healing and for this our Perfected women learned the lore of the mid-wife who helps women in labour of child-bed, so that they who were sick and those who laboured would be taught and shown the way.

We saw that the priests of Rome had become lustful men, both for women and for food; and they were thirsty for both wine and power and hungry for gold and for lordship over others. And this was not the way that the Master Jesus taught. But we were taught what the Master Jesus had taught. And that was to live chaste and honest lives, to love our brethren and to love God above all others. And so we lived and so we did.

And thus we died for our Belief at the hands of the corrupted priests. We died by many ways, but mostly we died by fire for that was what most rejoiced the hearts of those who would have us dead. For they scattered the ashes of those fires and of the true Believers and thought that they scattered our souls! But behold, the soul is not burnt by fire and neither can it be scattered as ashes. For the soul is immortal, as is made plain in this writing. For if my soul had been scattered, how could I make this woman write my chosen words? And it has been said, rightly, that a clean heart makes a merry head and a sound sleep and so it is; for indeed my heart is light and when I sleep, I sleep like a baby sleeps. And my body was burnt and my ashes were scattered but my soul lives!

And so let it be, for it is the Will of the Good God.'

This took up eighteen pages of A4 paper in the student note book that I kept near me; I was very surprised when I found it, and read it.
So I telephoned Llyn who listened and as soon as we could, arrange to we looked at it together. She recognized at once what it all meant. I at first thought that I should find and read as much as I could about the Cathars, but then I decided that it would be better not to do this, just in case more writing arrived. I did not wish to 'muddy the waters'.

<u>Notes written on January 11th 2007,</u> after I had been re-reading the 'writings':

That area where the Cathars flourished and blossomed most profusely was the richest part of that area which is now the South West of France, and is known as Langudoc Rousillon, but which was then made up of several independent states, or fiefdoms, which were governed by Counts, and was separate from France. This was the most enlightened and cultured area of Europe, where music and the arts flourished, where many ancient manuscripts were studied both by Cathars, other Christians, Jews and Muslims, in perfect amity.
What more joyous belief is there than that practised by the Cathars? The knowledge that this world – the world of the flesh – is actually 'hell'(the lowest level to which spirits can sink) means that when we leave this life of the flesh, we will be capable of living at a far higher, better and happier level than we can possibly know in material life. The land produced an abundance of vegetables, and fruit - especially grapes and olives; the rivers teemed with fish, (it was then believed that fish were not created by sexual means) as also did the sea around its shores. This land was perhaps not 'paradise' but it was a very pleasant place in which a soul could live, while in its 'robe of flesh' as the Cathar called the physical body. If this world was 'hell', how wonderful 'heaven' would be!
Is it not a very happy thought that when we leave behind our fleshly garments we shall be in a life more beautiful, much more filled with

love and light, than we can possibly dream of here?

Happiness must have abounded in the homes, villages and castles where the Cathars moved and worked: these were the 'Bons Hommes' and 'Bonnes Femmes' who healed bodies and minds, who raised up the fallen and gave hope to all.

These, in simple faith and the love of the Good God, were happy men and woman who were fearless – no 'hell' was greater than material life, and a heaven in which all was light and love was their eventual destination.

The Perfecti were abstemious and chaste, but although they were principally vegetarians and ate neither flesh nor dairy products, they enjoyed their vegetarian food, and the fruits and good wines of their country. They joined in the work and the celebrations of the people – singing, playing instruments and even dancing, for they were enjoined to be abstemious and celibate, not miserable! They did not force celibacy on their followers – indeed, had the entire community remained celibate there would have been no community!

What the Perfecti preached was love, understanding, and the equality of the sexes, and also of other religions; they preached with good humour in the earthy language of the country and their times. They did not use Latin, which only the highly educated used and which was not perfectly understood by a great many of the clergy, who daily used it in their Church Services, and they used simple words easily understood by the simplest of people; thus the population appreciated what they said and trusted them.

The criticisms levelled at the Cathars – that they were overly ascetic or that they denied the sexual nature of mankind, are gravely mistaken: the Perfecti were, in the main, recruited from people who had reached a certain age, who had experienced marriage and the joys and sorrows of life and who could therefore lay aside the desires of the flesh, usually with the consent of their partners. If through their ministrations as healers or by their teaching, both men and women came to accept the Cathar way of life and of belief, that was a crowning glory: but compassion was always the most important emotion. This does not mean that Perfecti turned their backs on their families and friends. Indeed, Love began at home, but radiated outward to all whom they met: 'Love one another' was the most important message that Jesus offered during his ministry; it was taken up with alacrity by the Perfecti who practised healing, and those Cathars who established schools, universities, hospitals and homes for the poor, the disabled and the widowed. For they understood that in these suffering prisons of flesh, dwelt spirits who came from God. God was Light; God was the Way; God was Good; and God, as brought by the Christ Spirit, through Jesus, was the Path that would lead all men to greater understanding, and eventually into a beautiful heaven.

The Cathars instituted something similar to a modern welfare state, in addition to which the population looked after each other as rural populations tend to do. Further, Cathar scholars studied
in companionship with other Christians, with Jews and with Muslims in the great Universities of the day thus gaining access to purely scholarly ans also to medical and engineering knowledge, for which Jews and Muslims from the eastern world werc famous. They were also able to benefit from the esoteric knowledge of these other Faiths, and a high degree of equality was exercised between scholars of all cultures; there was an understanding of different points of view that was well in advance of its time. Apparently, the most highly trained of the Cathars were enabled, by their grasp of esoteric matters, to appeal to the inmost spirit of those amongst whom they dwelt, taught, and healed. For Healing was of the greatest importance to them – Healing for both the suffering flesh and the entrapped, and therefore suffering, soul. Cathar Healers considered theirs to be the highest calling.

Sadly, there came a time when the Pope of the time instituted the 'Holy Office of the Inquisition': this was expressly to inquire into, and to abolish, Catharism and annihilate its followers.

Even to this day, the people of the area respect and revere these humble Good Men and Good Women who believed trustingly in the

Good God that they were prepared to die in the flames, rather than recant their belief. A.de G.

4 -   The Second Received Automatic Writings.

'There were certain scrolls and manuscripts, some on vellum, some on lesser skins and some inscribed on scrolls of papyrus, which is now called paper. And these elements were brought from many places, some from the Holy Lands and some from Rome and from Greece and others also were from Egypt where there still dwelt some of those of the Jewish faith, and some came from Spain from that part which was then inhabited by Moorish peoples. And those scholars whether they had been Jews, Muslims or Christians were full of the wisdoms which were not known to the Roman priests.

Many of the writings were methods of healing, such as herbs, surgeon's work, bone setting, and other kinds of healing.

But these scrolls also contained many truths which had been obscured by the Church of Rome, so that the people - even those of the lesser clergy – would never be able to have freedom to know the contents of these writings. But we had friends in many places, who valued the Truth for its own sake and who wished that the world should know of it, so they brought us these great treasures, which were beyond the price of gold or of precious stones. And of these scrolls and leaves we undertook to make fair copies so that they could be read by all who had the skill to read.

Yes, even the simple people of our Belief, because they had been taught to read and write in order that they might pass on to their fellows this wisdom and this knowledge. And the greatest benefit of these works was the love of the Good God for the true children whose souls belonged to the Good God, and who could learn love and the transience of the things of one lifetime.

And because there were often no priests in the villages and

homesteads in our lands, or because the priests that were there were self-seeking and demanded payment for the rites and sacraments of the Church of Rome, so it came about that many simple people had no priest to bless and baptise their children, or to unite them in marriage, or to consign their souls to the Good God when they died.

Therefore many a man and woman lived together in great love and harmony but without the blessing of marriage in the eyes of the Roman Church. And thus were they made sinners, and were so called. And yet the Good God, whose love is above all, recognized the love between these men and these women, and condemned them not. And so it was that one of these who so lived, when they received the call to Perfection they gave up the carnal part in their living, and although they continued in the home of their spouse in love, yet they slept aside from them, and lived as brother and sister in God. Still they succoured each other in true and pure love, and where there were children between them then they continued lovingly to provide for their offspring and to love and support them as father and mother should.

And while the Church of Rome called these man and women fornicators and their children base-born, yet the Perfected ones assured them that they did no sin and that their children were their true and rightful offspring, and that these children were their heirs and able to inherit all of what so ever was provided for them. And no man looked with shame upon the sons of such, nor barred those sons from marriage with true-born daughters. Also, the daughters of these unions of true love were dowered, and no man refused them marriage with their sons, for the lack of a marriage blessing from the priests of Rome, but saw that they were the children of truth, love, and loyalty. Yet this is not to suggest that the lack of chastity was honoured by those of the Belief, for it was not considered good to indulge in sins of lust with many women or with many men for that is wantonness and defiles the body and the mind and the soul.

For often there had been no priest present to make a marriage of these people.

And it happened oft times that both man and woman who had lived many years together by love alone joined, went forward in the True Belief and took the vows of the Perfected ones, and hence forward worked together for the well being of the souls of others.

When people, either men or women, were become Perfected, or were nigh to being Perfected, they were desired to go forth to all and to show by example and by truth of word and deed that the Faith that we followed was not corrupt as was the teaching of the priests of the Roman Church. For all who were Perfected lived as the Master Jesus had commanded them, with no concern for what they should have of the goods of this world, but relying on the Good God for both raiment and shelter and sustenance, they went forth with nothing but the book of St. John, a little bread, salt with which to pay those who helped them to food and shelter, and with the truth of the Good God blazing in their hearts.

So, too, did the knowledge that they had of the god of this world inform them, that they were able to make men and women, yes, and children too avoid the snares of Asmodeus whose intent is of evil and of power for his own dark ways. And thus many of these simple good folk went forth into the lands to show how Truth can light the dark places of the soul and can make well what is sick and corrupt. For I tell you now that the monasteries of the Church of Rome, not withstanding that there were indeed some saintly and scholarly men and women within their walls, had become sinks of iniquity and corruption, and their sins and dark deeds – yes, their treasons to those very flocks whose shepherds they had been appointed to be – cried out to heaven, and so to the Good God, as the stench of a turd disturbed by stirring with a stick, the which looks whole, but when so stirred up and enquired into, it stinks, and heaven itself is aware of the stink of it. And yet these priests and holy women cried out against us, and brought at last armed princes and knights against us. But these were encouraged by the lands that they could take from the righteous and true people, the believers; and the monies and treasures that they thought – though we were poor enough – that they could wrest from those who were condemned by the priests and lawyers of the Roman Church to die as outcasts and 'heretics'.

The whole of our Law was that we should serve only the Good God by whom all things were made leaving aside the lesser god of this world, who made not the world but who would try by his snares, to entrap men and women to his toils, so that he might seduce them away from the service of the Good God whose children we truly are.

Those who were Believers, whether they were of the nobility or whether they were poor labouring folk, went forth among their fellows, proclaiming everywhere the Glory and the Love of God. And at the proper times they gathered about the table, as did the family of the Master, Jesus - being his disciples and his brothers and sisters and his wife and children - and celebrated the Sabbath day with food and wine. So there came the Perfected and Believers together, breaking bread together and drinking wine and water. And this was a happy and a familial meeting. Thus many were brought into our Belief, because it was a happy and a modest Belief that required that each person should walk in the right way.

After supper was over, the women of the house took up any morsels of bread that the perfected ones had broken but had left uneaten. These crusts and morsels they wrapped in linen and when anyone was sick or like to die the women brought forth these morsels however old they were, and administered them to the sick person – and see, many were healed of their sickness or were raised up, so it was said, from their death-beds. This then was accounted miraculous, but in truth it was not the skill of the Perfected ones that healed them, nor the morsels of broken bread, but the Grace of God.

The Cathar Message
'Holy Bread'

We did not know they kept the crusts
when we had shared their simple fare –
those people we could truly trust
whose simple wish to have us there
was greater than their greed –
fortunes were offered for our lives,
and these were folk in need.
We were secure from lies and knives –
our secret safe with them –
and many women carried books
hid by their garments' hem.
And thus by wisdom and by stealth
our ministry we plied:
helping sick ones into health,
Consoling when they died.
Teaching always the simple creed
by which we lived –
                    For which we died.
And, after many years we learnt
that men had heard it said
folk kept crusts left by those who burned,
and called them 'Holy Bread'.

5 - Received Writing: An explanation of the beginning of Catharism

'We did not arise in our Belief out of spite for the Roman Church but rather to right the wrongs of the men and women in that church: for not only had they become themselves corrupted by money and power so that they were self indulgent, and ate well while their people went hungry, but also they had warped the work of the church. And that was something that we could not bear lightly. For we saw how men made the church work – not for God, but for themselves – and this was not the way of the holy ones who had been about the Master Jesus while he lived and worked in his life here on the earth. For his words and the words of John the Beloved were of light and of love. But in these dark days the priests who claimed to be of Jesus were anxious only to get goods and land and money from those who they should have helped: for did not Jesus say "Feed my sheep"? We believe that by this saying he meant all the men and women who followed his path of belief. But these 'shepherds' had become as wolves, ready even to devour their own sheep rather than to feed them and care for them. But we saw that there were other teachings as well as those of the Church of Rome and these teachings taught that no man should take from another unless it be offered in love. And no man could be turned into a 'god' when he was born of a woman and so was manifestly a man, as other men are.

And we were disgusted with the Mass, for the priests of Rome made claims which no man could accept: as, that the bread that they broke and the wine that they poured out did become by their hands the real body and also the blood of Jesus. So it would seem that every priest could make for himself a little Jesus of bread and wine.

And if Jesus could be made, and then made into a god, by the hands of a mere man, and one who was also a sinner, what sort of god could this be that they would have us serve?

For if the priest was corrupt then so must the god who was created by him be corrupt. Thus all who partook of that bread and wine, called "god", would be corrupted, for all corruption is a plague, spreading as all plagues spread. And if a man can make a god how is it that that god can then be greater than he who makes the god?

This was not the god who was served by the Hebrews, nor was it the god served by Jesus the Master who was a Hebrew, and who these corrupt men would have the people believe that they, the priests, had made before the faces of the people, and then asked the people to eat him.

And Jesus was an honest man and as he was always travelling, as we are taught, he was neither proud nor rich, and he spoke with all men that he met and women too, and this is not the way of the priests of Rome for most of them are too proud to speak with women, the poor, the out-cast, or the sinners. But Jesus taught that these were those whom his followers should love and care for, and seek to save.

And he healed the sick and he told his followers that they, too, could heal the sick as he did, either by the voice or by the laying on of hands.

For he said that whatever wonders he could himself do, still his followers could do more. Yet now the church has forgotten his teaching, and seeks rather to harm than to heal, to turn away rather than to encourage sinners back to grace.

We saw that it was a good thing to cast aside all that was mean and all that was unjust, and all that was not true.

And because the writers showed how that Jesus spoke to the people in the open air, so we made our professions and taught our teachings in the open air, rather than in built places. And we did not wear clothes embroidered in gold and in gems for certain it is that Jesus did not wear such rich garments when he walked through Judea or Galilee. And as he blessed and broke bread and took wine on the Sabbath so we, too, broke bread and took wine but as we knew that in his days it was the custom to mix the wine with water that it be not too strong so we too did, so that we did not become drunk with wine.

So revolted were our minds and bodies and especially our stomachs at the thought of eating flesh and blood that we ate no meat at all, so that we took no blood either. For who would eat that which he adored and that which was manifest to him as god?

Thus we did not celebrate the Mass as did those of the Church of Rome. Rather, when we gathered together in familiar places with those whom we knew and loved to take a meal with them and we shared bread and we shared a cup. And because this is a sign of friendship in all places, we set a dish of salt on our table whether it was in the forest or in a house or in a field.

And to learn to remember why we did these things we placed the book of St John on our table; we used that good book, full of wisdom, truth and light, to bless each other and to remind us of our duty to each other and to the Good God who made all our souls. And further to remind us, we said the prayer which we had learned.

And thus no one of us is more blessed than any other, but all can call his brethren to his table to feast together.

All who truly believe as we believe can come to Perfection. When this is so,and the have studied well, they can make their profession and take Consolamentum.

Which is that they must first be consoled by their brethren for the stains of sin on their souls, which souls are given to them by the Good God, so that they are made clean again by the recognition of their misdeeds and impure beliefs and they see that because these are grievous to them, they must be consoled and made whole again.

When this is done they may go forth, strong in faith and truth, to live and work in the knowledge of the Good God, aware of the snares of Asmodeus, the god of this world, and well able to avoid these.

Then as they strive at their work in this world, whether they be tillers of the soil, or bakers of bread, or as stewards to the lords temporal, or as lords themselves, they can teach by the words of their mouths and by the examples of their lives the Truth of the Good God and the untruths that have been done in his name. And if it be that they do well then it may be that this is their calling in the world, and they go forth, by twos, into the highways preaching the clean truth to whoso will listen.

They keep their bodies and their souls clean and chaste, taking no flesh, nor consorting in the pleasure of the flesh, but striving always to be good true men and women of God the Good and Great. So may they show other souls how to live and so may they themselves be Perfecti.

In the fire of Peace of the Good God are they cleansed, and the people see the light that streams from these Perfected ones and praise the Good God that they see it. And for this we did not need great buildings, for wherever blessings were given, that place was blessed. And especially we enjoyed being with the Good God amongst the trees.'

The Church of Trees.

'Among the trees of the Pays d'Oc
we made our church – not built by man –
to pray and praise and consecrate
with Holy Book and sacred Truth.
No great cathedral bright with glass
but tree trunks, ivy, moss and grass
our lichen-pillared glade arrayed.
And there, in innocence and Light,
our two-fold Faith we re-confirmed,
knowing we served the Lord of Light
and not the demon of this world.

Our life was simple, but not harsh –
Perfection did not cost us dear,
our diet plain but nourishing;
the ties of Love, though strict, were clear.
We had no difference of rank,
the shepherd and the lord were one –
the Parfait and the Parfaite both could be
of any rank or none, when once
the Book had rested on their head
and perfected their holy vows.

We met in open, windswept fields
and in amongst the forest trees –
no man had built our shrine!

Not made of common stone
our Church was flesh and bone,
our lowly rituals made
in open, friendly lands.
Peasant or lord could Perfect be
their station hindered not,
for love of God and fellow man
needs only holy honesty: as free
as wild flowers grow on mountain path.

When every place was dangerous to us
and houses could not hide us, then
into the woods and rocky places
we took our simple and our honest Faith
to pray in ways that made us free
for worship of the one Good God.
We knew there'd come a time
that trees no more could hide us:
when we were in such danger,
Then we fled :
'Tous a l'Ariège!' for secrecy.'

6 - Received Writing: Regarding Healing

'And touching the healing arts that the Perfecti learned: these were simple and homely but because the healers invoked the loving Spirit of the Good God, they were helped in this work.

And furthermore the Perfecti had learned from the manuscripts, brought from Egypt and other far places, which they studied. They learned that it is necessary to keep all clean where there are wounds or sickness, nor to let the wounded or sick lie in their filth but wash them, bathe their wounds and keep all cleanly about them. And having made all clean, open wounds should be washed with salt-water or with vinegar or, if not, then with wine and then bound in clean linen washed and wholesome.

For those pierced by arrows or other missiles or sword thrusts, they should be given poppy juice to drink, so that they may sleep a little, while the wound is searched and cleansed and sewn. And, this being done, then the wound is to be bound.

For those who have a bone broken, they must wherever possible be given poppy juice and if that is not available then some wine to ease them. Then may the injured bone be made straight and bound by strips of linen to a board or to a strong stout stick so that it grows straight together. And a dislocation or a train may be treated by the same method. But for the dislocation of a shoulder, the bladder of a goat or a pig should be placed under the armpit and filled slowly with water. And when the arm is so raised that it is again rightly placed, then, the water is to be let gently forth. And then the shoulder will be replaced with good success. This is painful. But it is a good feat of healing and does no damage of lasting effect to the joint.

There should be placed certain herbs in the room where the sick are: as lavender to sweeten the air. The oil of lavender will heal blisters of the feet and on the body. And marigolds made into balm will soothe burned skin. And yarrow will keep flies and other insects from the sick.

There are many herbs which may be used, as, nettles boiled and strained for disorders of the blood. And these are especially good for young women who have not their natural courses as they should.

Rosemary will soothe a headache, sage will comfort the bloat of the belly; buttercup roots made into a syrup with honey will help a cough that persists. Violet leaves made into a poultice with boiling water and laid between two pieces of linen and placed on the belly as hot as can be endured will ease the belly-ache. Rose hips, picked over and boiled will aid those whose blood is too thin, and there are many other simples – such as Solomon's seal root for bruises and speed-well for eye washes - too many to mention here. And honey laid to the wound will help the healing and prevent the rotting of the flesh.

But the main thing to remember is to wash the hands of the healer in warm water and cleanse them with soap-wort and dry them in clean linen towels, and to keep clean the sufferer – for more die of dirt infesting their sick bodies and rotting them than die of their hurt or sickness. The linen of the bed they lie in must be clean and that room free of dust, dirt, soiled rushes, dogs, cats and any other creatures whose hair will fall out and carry infection from the sick, and fleas. The floor shall be well washed with clean water daily and more often if the sick should vomit.

The clothing of the sick must be likewise clean and well

washed; and the Healer must wash hands before and after attending each patient – and to this end a basin and ewer and towels should be carried by an apprentice, following the healer in every place and watching to see and learn.

And for leprosy and other disorders of the skin and bone, there should be not rushes or sand or any other thing upon the floor, and that floor should be washed with clean water and a broom branch three or four times daily with cleansing herbs in the water. And the clothes and linen of the sufferers must be especially well washed and passed over heated irons that no infection remain in them. Or they can be boiled in water in a large pan and then kept bubbling for some long time so that the infection is boiled out of those garments that may touch the afflicted parts.

And there is another way of Healing which uses neither simples nor herbs. And this Healing is by the Spirit and is the laying on of Hands. Now this may best be done by appointing a time and a place where the sufferer and the healer can remain private together.

And it matters not a whit whether the sufferer lies down or sits or stands. The room should be light and, if possible, with air blowing through it but not cold, for the comfort of the sick and afflicted person. And then the healer will make a peaceful place in their heart and mind, asking for the Grace of God's Healing Love to flow through his hands or her hands. Often there is no need to touch the afflicted upon their body, for the healer will see the light around the body and where they see no light, there is the sickness.

And some will feel the sickness at a distance of about a man's hand, as a tingling in his or her hand or as a heat rising from the afflicted. Then can the healer direct the flow of the Spiritual Love into that part of the body where they feel the presence of the affliction. And when the sensation in the hands ceases then the healing has been accomplished

There is another method of healing that is especially effective between two that are Perfecti. And this is in this wise: that they shall both be of the same sex, for that hands will be laid on, which is not seemly between men and women. And the afflicted will tell the healer where the ailment is. Then the healer will make a peaceful place in his or her mind, so too will the sufferer. And this place will be filled with the Light of the Love of the Good God. And when they feel that Light strong, the Healer will place the palm of the right hand above that part that ails and the palm of the left hand below that part that ails. And as the hands become hot then the Healing begins. And when the Healing has been accomplished the hands will return to their accustomed feeling.

Now this may be used for others than Perfecti but then it must be done with a third person in attendance and this for the sake of seemliness.

And in case of the ailment being not in the main body it can be done between men and women, but where it is in the main body then it must be a man who so treats a man, and for a women a woman.

And it is said that all Perfecti may cure any ailment in another Perfecti, whatsoever the ailment may be, by this method.

For it is by the will of the Good God that this healing takes place. This method may be employed between believers, but is most efficacious between Perfecti I do not know the reason this should be, but all manner of pain and ills have in this way been made whole. And if this be necessary then the roles may be reversed and the healer may be healed by that one who has just by them been healed.

And this kind of healing is not a secret healing, yet it is better to be kept private between believers. Yet whatsoever method of healing is employed, the hands must be washed both before and after so that a certain period of time is set for the healing and it is finished cleanly.

And all the rest of the healing which is learnt by the Croyants is the use of simples, as the old folk of the countryside have used these many years. Yet these were never before made into a written list nor inscribed in a parchment so that many pieces of good knowledge and wisdom were lost with the end of the earthly life of those who had studied them.

Now sound too may be Healing. For some sounds, as the sound of doves cooing may be restful to the afflicted and cause a respite in pain. And much blue should be about the sick for the same reason that blue is the colour of the sky and brings peace into the heart. For oft-times it is disorder in the the heart or brain which causes the sickness rather than illness or wounds in the body. And these troubles of mind and spirit are in as much need as are the ills of the body temporal.

And the main thing that the healer requires, is a perfect trust in God and without that trust is nothing accomplished.

And referring back to sounds in the manner of healing, it may be that certain resonances of sound will echo through the bones of the sufferer and induce a faster knitting of broken bones. For I have heard it said that the singing of boys, which is peculiarly sweet and high, gives a vibration that sets at ease both heart and mind, soul and body. But this I have not yet attempted, being but a simple healer and using my known and tested methods of healing.

Now the Roman priests tell their adherents to call upon the saints to heal them, using bones and other relics to this purpose: but these relics are often found to be false relics, and how will a chicken bone heal a broken leg or a wound inflicted by an arrow?

Therefore there is more reason to use the means which are known to work well, such as cleaning and sewing wounds and reducing fevers by the use of willow-bark boiled and pounded. Yet this last must be discreetly employed or the blood will flow too freely and the sufferer may die of a bloody flux. And the sick should be encouraged to drink much water and that boiled and cooled, that their fever be abated and the humours of the body cooled and made sufficient.

 And every healer should beware that there are those who will claim the illness is of the body when the illness is of the soul, the brain or the heart. And thus must the healer closely question the sick to ensure that the answer given is true.

Furthermore, everyone who would prepare salves, ointments and medicines should first acquaint themselves with those plants and roots which are poisonous, like aconite, night-shade and other herbs and plants whose juice, flowers and roots are not safe unless in the hands of one experienced for many years in the healing Arts, for otherwise the sick one may die and the healer loose not only reputation but life also. And often it is plants which please the eye and gladden the nose which are the most poisonous – as are bluebells which look and smell fair and lovely but whose juices are not readily to be taken.

Therefore be warned that it is a long apprenticeship and study. And those who heal the sick should put a dalmatica of clean linen over their gown a to be changed daily and let them essay to be cleanly in necessity too.'

It would seem that 'cleanliness is next to Godliness' was a strict tenet for the Good Christians, even so long ago.

7 - Some Questions and Answers

On August 5th, 2003, a piece of writing appeared, in response to a request made by Llyn:

'I came to speak to you because you asked me to do so – you had a need for me to do so.
I am aware of your hurt and your discomfort: it is however less than that which you suffered in that other time, so long ago, when it seemed that the whole world appeared in arms before you, and we were all sacrificed to our belief. You have memories of many lives: there are others of which you have no recall, for in so many of them you were just a simple man or woman of no importance, no significance. Yet your lives were still needed. It is not necessary to be famous or even doing great works for your life to be worthwhile.
Just as a stretch of sand is made up of millions perhaps billions of tiny grains, even so is humanity and its work made of many small lives. If these are well lived they give stability and gravity to the world of men. But your interest runs further than the world of man, for you look to the stars, to the sun and moon, and beyond, to where there are mysteries too great to comprehend. Your work now, all the good that you have done, all the pity and kindness that you have shown, lend ballast to the sum of life lived in human form.
Now the world has once more turned its back on goodness, decency, prudence, wisdom and love: so it is imperative that the Higher Power gather all those of good will together. Your love and wisdom and concern are needed, but you must not be hard on yourself – reflect – a happy man, a good home, happy, well adjusted children are riches beyond price. If you

did nothing else, you would have given these gifts to the world.

At present you are bruised: were you not bruised before? Those who awaited for you at the field of Montsegur that day were in no way gentle: you have felt the injuries inflicted upon you at that time. Yet you went singing and confident to your physical death. Today you are not required to die for what you believe to be true! You are required to live a life of quiet devotion to your family and friends and a willingness to attend to those who are less blessed than you. And this is the real path up the mountain! Tread carefully and all will be well.

You asked my blessing – it is freely given. "Roger Isarn".'

On October 7th, 2013

Llyn asked this question of Bishop Guilhabert de Castres, during a session of Mediumship:

'One of the confusions that I have in my mind is about time. As we understand time in a human sense, there is no such thing in the spirit world, and therefore the confusion in my mind is about how past lives and today's lives are lived – how does it work, what are the mechanics? '

Answer:

'Spiritual growth is open to all souls, but not all souls will wish to proceed. Many repeat and repeat and repeat the same errors in judgements, decision making processes and responses to certain events to the point where they almost, but not quite, draw such events to themselves – like attracting like - as is so in universal law. Others, seeking always to learn and move on and expand their knowledge and their souls, rejoice in watching their souls grow and brighten with light after each attempt.

So you understand that some choose to stay static, some seek always the light, and choose to evolve.

And because all human souls have free will, they have the right to choose. Some people do the most appalling things for the very best of reasons and others the best of things for the worst of reasons: but, again, it is their right to make that choice.

However there is never a time when no-one is carrying a sheet of reckoning, because always the soul is accountable for the choices and decisions that it makes. There is no judge and there is no jury, but the soul is eventually its own judge and jury.

As to time, there is no such thing, but the vastness and expansiveness of eternity is so great that mere mortals cannot grasp so enormous a concept. The in breathing and the out breathing of the cosmos, of God if you will, stretches across such vast expanses as to be immeasurable by human view. Human beings view this as eternity because they do not have the capacity to measure the vastness.

In seeing time in an expanded form of billions of years, the age of this present universe is only a glimpse of reality.

As to your question of time, you have science in modern days and science talks of the laws of physics. While science and scientists consider provable facts about the behaviour and nature of reality, some progressive and deep thinkers in your time take a step back and try to see the bigger picture.

They call this view of science "quantum physics".

Quantum Physics has fundamental laws in the same way that physics has, but these laws can step outside 'reality' and look at theory. Theoretically they say there are multi-dimensions both of time and space, and multitudinous life forms.

To put this in a nut shell, if you can think of something and perceive it, then it will exist somewhere. This because thought is creative and the higher thinking creatures can create their own reality.

This is what quantum physics says.

To some extent this is true. There are many human arguments – man has thought of God, therefore God exists – did God exist before man thought of God? These puzzles, these questions are the theoretical guidelines of quantum physics.

And yet, look around you, and at what you know of the known world.

Look at the fundamental operations of the mediums. How are they able to see into the unseen? How are these mediums able to converse with those who do not live now? How are they able to know what is not known and to share their reality of the world? Mediums are individuals who have slipped into the quantum world and who have brought that information back to the normal reality, to share it. Mediums are not particularly gifted in comparison to all other human beings, but they are developmental. Think of them as a prototype for what human beings will become next. Because the laws that drive evolution do not cease simply because Charles Darwin thought of them, but they drive life forward – to what conclusion, you may ask. When? Where? How? That remains to be seen. Meanwhile, we continue to exist at the same 'time' and at many levels, and can exchange ideas. Does that satisfy you?

October 11th, 2013.

Another question from Llyn:

'Can energies enter a person sometimes for their good, but most times it seems, not so good? Can you give some guidance as to the question and how to deal with such energies?

Bishop Bertrand Marty, answered her:

'The word 'disease' takes many forms, has many different expressions. Disease is an alteration in the function of the physical body or the mental capacity. Some causes are through infection, some cases are self inflicted and some are through invasion of the body from external forces. There are many different forms of disease; all of these bring about the failing in the health of the individual. Infection and invasion are not necessarily the same thing.

The power of the human mind is great but with all great things there are also disadvantages, flaws, if you like. Human beings have great capacity; they also, unfortunately, suffer from great stupidity and don't have self awareness to the degree, perhaps, that they should. They don't have the advantage of exercising control very often. In our day we believed so much in the importance of the training of the mind, to reach its own potential. To strengthen the body and to strengthen the mind, is to strengthen the spirit.

Body invasion comes in the form of infection; mind invasion comes in the form of self doubt, and spirit invasion comes from an external source.

We are capable of self healing, but very rarely is that exercised to its full capacity; and so we train those who are gifted in the arts of healing so that they can assist those that are less able. Many, through mistakes and errors – poor judgement - leave themselves open up either physically, emotionally or spiritually, to invasion or to infection. Much can be done to help these individuals; much can be done to train those that are skilled, to assist them, but marrying up the two is not always the easy part. Many suffer in silence and no assistance comes to them because of their silence; others are not aware of the intensity of their suffering and because they suffer in silence they themselves are not aware that there is help that they could access.

Healers of all types, formal and informal, professional and amateur, look always for those they can help but they do not necessarily find them – those that are in greatest need.

For a spiritual invasion a spiritual doctor, to advise and guide, is extremely useful to instruct those healers to work with the spirit doctors to effect change. For those patients who are suffering emotional problems, self doubt and the like, physicians who are qualified in that form of service, -counselling and therapy, are most advantageous to the patient; and those who manifest physical disease very often do so because their immune system has been depleted from onslaughts in other areas. While areas can be strengthened through therapeutic help, the specific healing techniques for specific problems are the most effective. In our experience, sadly, with all matters to do with healing, you can lead a horse to water but you cannot make him drink. Some people can have help all around them, and also support, but they will not take it.

Now we come to the great spiritual questions. When souls manifest in the physical world they come here to learn and also to experience that which they cannot experience in the world of spirit. So while they are here they try things out. Some things are to their advantage, and some things are very definitely to their detriment – but they will try them, because that is why they are here – to experience. And so you see the very best healers, the finest level of help and support, can be available to those who suffer. If they will not avail themselves of it, what is anyone to do? It is possible that these souls have chosen that way in which to learn.

To learn what, you may ask: to learn compassion for others

who suffer. To learn the difference between good and evil, and to recognize at a profound level the natural laws that govern the spirit world. Perhaps those individuals that suffer now intend to come back and give healing to those who are suffering on another occasion.

The great plan for all of this is so vast that we cannot possibly grasp it. All we can do is learn the laws: the natural laws that govern each plane of being, and adhere to those laws in the best way we can because the laws will not bend and they will not change: it is we who must adapt and learn within natural law, within spiritual law, within God's Law.'

Another question from Llyn:
'Do you have something further to say about addiction?'

Answer:
'What most clear thinking and compassionate people will see in addiction is an overwhelming drive on the part of the suffering individual to self harm.

Any alcoholic who is intent on self harm will elect slow suicide and drink them selves to death – drink alcohol until the body can take no more and begins to break down.

Drug addiction is even more toxic because of the nature of the constructed drugs that are used; not natural drugs from the plant world, man-made drugs that devastate the body in ways that natural materials do not.

So why should somebody elect to self harm in such a way? Our understanding of this is that self harming is not a suicide attempt; it is actually an escape attempt. So many elements are brought to bear in such situations, but it almost always begins with violence: violence to the sufferer, whether that violence be physical, verbal, mental or spiritual, and the individual will have experienced that violence – profound violence – at some level. The younger that person when they experience it, the greater the likelihood that they will turn that harm upon themselves instead of out upon the world.

When it is turned on to the self, self-harming behaviour begins to form and it is very hard to break that pattern, because self harm begins to become a means of release in the mind of that person - their escape from the hellish place where all this suffering exists. And so they seek ways to escape, self inflicting more and more harm upon their own souls until they can finally escape and be released back to the world of spirit.

This self destructive course does at first seem like madness, but it is a vehicle for change. If the person was expressing the other side of the coin and was perpetrating violence out onto the world instead of onto the self, the devastating effects would be very far reaching and the number of lives affected, the harm done, the suffering inflicted, would be far more.

In a perverse way, self harm is shielding others from the worst effects of the violence the individual is suffering. Do you understand better now?

Addiction is a noxious thing but it is not an entity in its own right. It is a manifestation of great harm and violence perpetrated on the individual sufferer. Now, we come to the nub - the violence does not necessarily come from this lifetime. It can come from previous lifetimes, and never having been resolved, can be carried forward into the present life; never the less the harm of it is just as devastating.

This affords a whole different interpretation of the understanding of the victim and the aggressor. The victim who has self harmed has turned the violence in upon himself; the aggressor is turning the violence out, into the world. They are bedfellows, either sides of the coin, the heads and tails of the coin; it is from the same cause and it brings us back to what people understand to be good and evil. We call that which causes harm 'evil' and that which causes goodness 'good'. But many have meant well but caused great harm, and many have intended appalling harm, but only good has come of what they have done.

Think of a clear, small pool and one rain drop landing in the pool, the ripples spreading out from where the drop fell. Even after the waves have passed to the edge of the pool, they turn back on themselves and come to the centre, and then back out to the edge again, weakening all the time. Thus it is with violence, wherever it is manifest, who-so-ever's life it touches, it has the same debilitating effect. And so you see, when you witness someone suffering self harm, you see only a fraction of the story. There is the greater, deeper story underneath, then it ripples out and affects many in its process'.

October 21st, 2013

Llyn asked a question of Bishop Guilhabert de Castres:
'I am interested in the question of sin, and whether there are influences let loose in our world: are sin and evil, concepts of man or a real force in the world'.

The answer:
'I can give you only an opinion, but you must remember that you have asked a Cathar, and our beliefs were very strong and dearly held! When we passed from this world to the spirit world many of our beliefs were brought into question, because from Spirit one can see the bigger picture; and so we have evolved and have modified some of the ideas we had in past times. However, I will do my best to answer you. A particular

school of thought is that of Buddhism, which believes that there is this world, of the here and now, and other realms, the worlds of Spirit. That belief also encompasses automatic reincarnation.

In our day we had names for those who have a guiding influence over both realms.

We believed that the higher realms were ruled by that which we called The Good God, a divinity that is pure, refined, compassionate, and ultimately the source of all life.

In the physical world there is another deity a lesser god, if you will. We called this the Fallen One. He had once, it was believed, lived in the higher realms with the One True God, but, believing himself to be greater and more powerful and influential than the True God, he fell from grace, and as his spirit weighed more and more heavily, he found that he could no longer exist in the higher realms, and when he finished his downward journey, he found himself in the physical world.

We called this lesser deity Asmodeus, the Fallen One.

We understood that sin does not exist in the higher realms of Spirit because temptation does not exist there.

All beings in the higher realms are completely immersed within the influence of the sublime Light of Divinity.

In the physical world that is not the case. In the physical world temptation is all around because Divinity has created humanity with free will: the right to make choices in this world, and the physical world has become an entrapment. If you think about this in terms of light and dark, - and to use the Eastern term Yin and Yang, the two great forces of the universe then if either were to cease to exist, so would the other also, because the balance needs both – good and bad, light and dark – both are necessary – else what is there? One action only is not choice And thus as sad as the physical world is, and as cruel as it can be and as dangerous as it can be, the human being always has choice. And because of that, the dark one must exist in order for there to be variety, so that choice exits.

To look at it in another way, the physical world, created by the Divinity is like a school and each cell that manifests in the physical world does so to learn.

Some of that learning is joyous and some of it is bitter; some of it is hard, some of it is beautiful; but it is the choice of the individual as to what they choose to explore.

And so, in ancient times, the teachers taught that there was good and evil, that there was God and a devil. As an allegory it was a way in which to help people to understand light and dark and the concept of choice and of personal responsibility, both to self and to others.

Very often individuals will pursue a path that is fraught with danger, and we say that they have a 'devil may care' attitude: they court danger, they court sadness - they court the dark side, if you wish but with every action they eventually learn from that which they make.

Mankind has always struggled to understand war, death, misery, famine, disease – all the horrors of the physical world - which do not exist in the Higher Realms. But where has all this misery come from? And because we comprehend the concept of divinity of the great creative force of God, as we said 'the Good God'. And if the Good God created all that is beautiful and pure and of the light, the inevitable question is – what created the darkness, the ugliness, the disease and the famine? Thus the concept of the devil began to be formulated in the minds of mankind as a means to explain the evil that exists in the physical world. But is it evil as such?

As I said to you, we have formulated and refined our ideas over time, and we have come to the conclusion that the devil is a mask a persona created to explain the harsh reality of the physical world. Does a devil exist? No, we doubt it.

Is there much suffering in the world? Oh, yes, there is that indeed, there is that! But humans will always relate their view to how it affects them as individuals and as groups of human beings, and they don't stop to think about the suffering in the animal kingdom, the suffering of the plant kingdom or the suffering of the planet itself: much of that suffering is man-made, not devil-made. So sin is questionable.

Remember:good men cause bad things,and bad men can cause good things

Is there light as well as dark force in the universe? We believe there are opposites and that those opposites co-exist. Is that helpful?'

Llyn:

'Yes, it is, thank you. I just wonder, because you touched on this question. That is, if the devil is a mask, in other words an artificial concept that has been created by man to explain the things that are not good, and you spoke of temptation: when does that arise? Is that in the mind of man – to create good thoughts and bad thoughts?'

Answer:

'It is most likely to be in the hormones of mankind, because human beings are governed so entirely by the chemical markers in their bodies, which cause change – for example during puberty. Children are innocent of many of the vagaries of adult life. If they are left to their own devices they are usually sublimely sweet. When they enter adolescence a great change comes over them: by the time they are adults the question of good and evil, light and dark, sin and goodness, suddenly becomes a very real quandary. So what is it that causes this change when there is the movement into adulthood from childhood, which is governed entirely by the chemicals in the body? It is very likely that this is a uniquely human question. As to the rest of life on the planet – it goes about its business without intellectual worry, if you understand my meaning.'

Llyn:
'So what you are saying is that within the human being there are chemicals which will affect the way that people think and then, because thoughts are very powerful, affect the way in which they behave?'

Answer:
'Yes. Adult behaviours are driven by human physiology. When it is combined with intellect it can create all sorts of problems. Human beings are extraordinary animals – we are not separate from the natural world, we are part of the natural world and when we come from Spirit into matter we must accept the whole parcel. The majority of adult human woes are caused by missing a chance to reconcile the purity of spirit with the much more dense physical reality of the natural cycle of the physical world. The dilemma is:- are we human beings learning to be spiritual, or are we spiritual beings learning how to be human? My Cathar brothers and sisters believed the latter rather than the former and that is what the great struggle that incarnating into the physical world is all about.

We believe it is not just a spiritual question but a question that can be answered by the higher philosophy. The world of Spirit is of a very high frequency, very refined, very pure, and that what does not manifest there cannot do so because of its intrinsic density.

As we lower our vibration, our vibrations become denser: in

order for a spiritual being to manifest in the physical world, its vibrational frequency must change in that way.

So the pure part of the human being the refinement, the light of the human being, is the soul that, thanks be to the Good God we bring with us when we re-incarnate to remember where we come from and what our Source is.

Becoming encapsulated within a physical body lowers the vibration to such a density that we cannot but be absorbed into the physical world -- and then the struggle truly begins.

But it is not a struggle for life as physical creatures understand it, it is a struggle for the survival of the refinement of the soul whilst it is embodied because we learn lessons when we come here and the great test is to learn from them, retain them, and when we return to spirit, to carry that teaching with us so that we have gained from the experiences and grown through them rather than having been impoverished by it.

So many human beings do not yet understand that incarnation is part of the cycle.

Some Eastern peoples do have evolved concepts of this – they call it 'Karma' - but the majority of western peoples, being now largely monotheistic do not grasp the spiritual reality of human life on earth. Human beings are most extraordinary creatures and their capacity and ability far exceeds any other life form, but they squander it, they misunderstand it, they do not develop it. We tried to teach this truth, through our great movement – and many heard and followed, and tried to grow though their embodied experience, but by far the majority did not grasp it. And so when we have the opportunity to share this great teaching we always try to do so.'

Bishop Marty had this to say when Llyn asked about "Group Souls"

'This is the movement of groups of souls through relatively long periods of time: their history is more about what binds them together as a system of belief. As groups of friends come together to share similar interests, so groups of souls come together to explore particularly interesting and rewarding endeavours from a soul point of view. So they have a common goal, a common belief.

At the highest level the evolution of their souls is a promise they have made to do a particular piece of spiritual work, which is almost always about service to others.

Imagine, if you will, that a long time ago a group of people came together and shared a religious belief, an intellectual understanding, an emotional commitment to serving others with a particular focus and drive, to the point where these souls were prepared to give up almost everything to do with their own selfish interest and gain for the sake of the higher spiritual purpose.

That aim and that goal have no beginning and no ending.

It is the alignment of souls, by an act of will, to a higher purpose – the service and development of others. If those individual souls pass away and make their transition and they do not believe their task to be complete, when they have the opportunity to return to an earth-life they bring the same drive, commitment and focus with them. They don't remember their previous life immediately, because souls are not permitted to have full recall of their previous incarnation, but they are evolved enough to recognize they have an inner drive, and when they meet others with an identical drive there is recognition – a coming together, and the joy of sharing again that higher goal. And so they will work steadfastly together for that aim and for that same goal.'

Writing found in September 2001, in response to the question 'How shall we account for reincarnation if more people are born than people die?'

Answer from an unknown Source:

How will souls be furnished to new people born living, if fewer people have left their old bodies?

Behold the answer to this mystery: at no time are more bodies born on earth than have previously lived on the earth. What think you? That the Good God cannot make an infinite number of new souls if he should will it so? Just by His breathing forth His thoughts and His Will, he made this world and all that exists. And by His breathing forth His will were the archangels and angels of light made, and so, too, the angels who have now grown dark. For God is the One Beginning, the Alpha and Omega. And the Good God made all that is, and all the power (now called energy) that exists.

Each soul, angel or human, must decide how they will employ this energy whether for furthering the Light, or to misuse light and follow the path that envelopes their souls in darkness.

Now those who choose to follow Asmodeus, the ruler of this passing world, have to return, after their lifetime, into a new body, thus to redeem their former misdeeds and mistakes. And this they will be forced to do until the light of truth dawns on them and they see clearly that they must purge their former misguided lives and seek the Light.

Those who know in their inmost souls that they must seek the Light of the Truth of the Good God, will seek, during all their life on Earth, to do that which is good, both for their fellow men and for their own salvation and they will seek far above the things of this world, and they will learn to live in the Light of the Good God, so that when their times of learning have been encompassed, then they will be rejoined to each other and to the one Great Spirit, the Good God who made them.'

Writing Received on 9th June, 2003:

'To my brothers and sisters: Greeting!
I have heard it said that those of our Faith believed that at the time of physical death our souls, if there was no human body in which to dwell, and if they had not been Consoled and reconciled, would live in the body of a horse, or a dog, an ass, or some other creature. But this is false. This is an untruth told to make us appear foolish and to discredit our teachings.
The priests of Rome have many times said many things about us: namely that we were weavers, liars and unchaste men and women, heretics and sorcerers: they never named us fools! For many times have we debated with their scholars and many times have our arguments defeated them.
And is it not foolish to say that Good Christians would believe that a spirit emanating from the Good God, part of the Spirit of God, would dwell in a beast? The Good God has devised spirits for the beasts and for all living things and they are not the same as the spirits of men and women.
It is not from the fear of devouring other human spirits that we refrain from eating flesh or the products of unchaste union. We refrain from eating flesh and the products of procreation because we know that the spirits of men and women need reconciliation and Consolation, so that they may return to the Good God to be reunited with that Spirit.
Therefore we partake of no basely produced food for there are vegetables and fruits, nuts and berries and even fish, that are not impurely conceived and that will not pollute our bodies and our spirits. This is the reason for our abstinence. All other

reasons are stories spread to make us appear foolish.

Now, as to our great and sacred rite, the Consolamentum: You will find versions of this, but few, all too few, proceed from writings of ours that have come down to your days for in spite of our efforts, so many have been lost.

The Consolamentum was administered to those Believers who were dying, to those who had pledged to live perfectly by our doctrine for all their days.

This Rite was performed simply, for the spirit was reconciled and restored by the laying on of hands, the recitation of the Book of John, the Bearer of Light, and by the repetition of the prayer known as the Pater Noster, and by confession of sin. Then would we encourage the spirit telling it that it had been reconciled and consoled. Then the spirit could dwell once more in the body in which it had chosen to dwell, and which had become purified in order that it might receive that spirit. And at the death of that body the Consoled spirit would find the way back to reunion with the Spirit of the Good God.

Yet it was necessary that those who consoled were themselves purified and reconciled with their spirits, for otherwise the Rite was in vain.

Now Brothers and Sisters, in your days there are few who make ready; for they eat meat and other unclean foods, and they do not listen for the voice of the Good God. Then might the god of this world claim them for his own, so that they must be conceived again as denizens of this world.'

8 - Received Writing: Concerning the local population's support for the Cathars

'Now many great and influential lords and ladies, and men and women powerful in these regions were believers – indeed some of their ladies, widows and the unmarried sisters of their houses, were Perfected women and with their dowers they built houses for women to be safe in. The power of these men and women kept us mainly safe from the prying eyes of Rome; yet they could not always befriend and defend us. If our lords could not help us, we were hidden by poor good folk or else we took to the mountains and the forests for these places were well known to us, and moreover we could easily mingle with the common people, labouring beside them so that no-one could guess who we were from our habit or demeanour; and the calluses on our hands hid that we were also scholars and had wisdom.

Many noble families had been Believers for many generations for that they had found out the iniquities of the Roman priests and the shame and sham of the religion which these had taught them. And so trusting to the good sense of their countrymen, and seeing that we led honourable, truthful lives, not corrupted and deformed of heart or mind, they gladly followed the path of Truth hiding us in their households when searches were made for us; and so we were protected by the great houses. It was from these nobles that we were provided not only with money for things for which we stood in need, but also with sergeants to guard us, should need arise, for all these nobles then had retinues of men, trained, armed, and able. These sergeants at arms often became Believers, since being with us they saw that what we preached, we practised, and that what we claimed we lived by. And that which we lived by was the true message of Jesus – that not a sparrow falls, but the Good God knows of it, yes, even to a little tiny bird. Yet they were still able to defend us, not having professed the true faith and belief and become Perfected. And when the last battle came at the siege of Montsegur many of these men, and their women-folk, both wives and daughters and sweethearts, took the Consolamentum, and at last died with us to this earthly life, in the fires of the Roman priests and their minions.

Not only the sergeants served in the siege – their womenfolk also learned skills of cleanliness and healing and worked hard to the Glory of the Good God, especially one or two of them, who found that they could heal by the help of the Spirit; and those women also went with us to the fire, but we taught them and also the sergeants to withdraw from the body, which will show that it was not only the learned who could perform this act of withdrawal, but men and women from the fields could also learn this discipline for themselves.'

The Cathar Message
'In The Field'

We stood together;
back to back;
needing no tether;
garbed in black.
Watching with open eyes
the faggots rise.
We saw the torch
They brought to light
our martyrs' pyre –
we did not fight,
but we sang higher
above the crackling flames
and as the people prayed,
calling each of our names,
we left the scorching heat:
our spirits, taught to rise,
were garnered as the wheat
in Perfect sacrifice.
Our bodies burned.
Our souls were free;
And people learned
That they, as we,
Could conquer still:
The Church of Trees
Is where they will!

On Wednesday March 16th, 1244, 225 Cathars both Perfecti
and Believers, men and women, old and young, were burned
by the 'Holy Office of the Inquisition', after the capitulation of
the Cathar fortress of Montsegur.

9 - Received Writing: Touching the simplicity of Catharism.

Found on September 10th, 2001:

'It was not hard to obey our Teaching, it was as simple as the Master himself taught it: love the Good God and your fellow man, and love your neighbour as yourself. Seek to build faith and truth and good works, not to destroy. Show how people may place faith in good works, mostly by Love. For how could an old man, laid in his bed, penniless and cared for by his family, help any other soul? Yet he can! For by his gentle wisdom in his wise acceptance of his present weakness he can give others the opportunity to do good works.

Likewise, he can give a pattern of patience and faith in the Good God; so can we, whether we are in health or in sickness, show by our example that there is nought in this world of flesh that we may not face and conquer. No, not even the physical death itself can overcome a spirit made strong by Love and Truth. For the Truth is that we continue to live in as many lives as the Good God sees fit to set us in: in each lifetime we learn more of the Truth of this life, which is of the Good God.

And so will come the time when no more learning for this life is needful. Then all good souls will come together at one time and in one place, and when all are accounted and present, the Lord of Eternal Life will make known to us how He will deal with us and with all souls. And so, until that day we shall dwell here in learning and in the love of mankind's souls and of the Truth of the Good God, whose will shall prevail over the demons of this world. And then shall the Lord of Light reveal all to us, and to all his children, both listening, and sleeping, over all the lands of this world.'

Writing Found on September 20th, 2001.

'Has not even the lowliest of men often wished that he might be lifted up, perfected, made free, would any not wish to rise from the mire and drudgery of daily life, to reach the heavens? And is not this a clear indication that the soul is not part of the garment of flesh – the body – that becomes its dwelling place on earth?

Among the sons of men are those who sing and who make songs, and those who lift their souls and hearts in love.

Too often this love is for a woman – a lady to whom they dare not aspire but who represents all purity and all beauty and truth. Such are the troubadours who go amongst mankind singing. And if they but knew it, the lady of their delight is the personification of their own soul, which seeks to leave the earth and to return to the Good God, and to the state of Grace which they have presently lost. Their beloved is our Truth!

Yet by the grace and love of the Good God these suffering souls may yet be saved and returned to that same Good God and when this happens, light shines on them.

These illuminated souls are apparent to those who know the true Light, and these souls, who are recognized by them, may be approached and offered the way to be Perfected. If this state and this training for this state, is accepted, the enlightened ones become one of the Perfecti – the teachers, healers, and comforters of any who approach them sincerely seeking for the Truth. Their training includes, at the right time, the separation of the pure and spiritual self from the corrupt physical garment which on earth it is their lot to wear. This withdrawal may be called upon in extreme danger or necessity but it is mostly confined to the time immediately before physical death, when the Consolamentum has been requested and performed.

The correct time and way for this is close to the obvious end of material life, at this time only medicine and water are administered to those who suffer fatally, and is the final preparation for the new life in the spirit world.

Lucky and favoured are those who knowing that their earthly life is drawing to a close can call upon this knowledge to assist them to find their rightful place, in peace, with the Good God.'

Received Writing Found in October, 2001

'In the days when we roamed our native fields gathering our sheep, which were the souls of our compatriot brothers and sisters, we were most careful to speak discreetly, being unobtrusive as we possibly could, and to do good by what stealth we might. In these days too, good Brother, we must keep alert for those who claim to be of our number but who are ready to steal our knowledge, our Truth, and use it to our detriment. Therefore be wary of those who claim much but who can substantiate nothing for these are deluded folk who strive ever to stir up troubles and disbelief, and to bring down upon the heads of True believers the wrath of the established church and the state.

Therefore we urge you to be wary, to be guarded and to probe deeply before you accept any word from one unknown to you, who has not been tried in the fire of faith. For many will claim association and membership of our Faith and Truth, merely for their own aggrandisement. Others will do so in order to harm the true Perfects and their successors and students. Stay mindful, therefore, of the dangers that you court and the possible result of too much trust.

You have every means at your disposal to test those who profess to know and believe, but mistake us not, for we know the weakness of the human heart.'

A Received Writing: July 30th, 2003.

'And neither the Good God nor his Christ, His representative, could be born of man and woman as a being of Spirit, and not of common clay. For the god of this world fashioned man from the clay to make robes of flesh in which to imprison souls. The priests of the Roman Church have said that the son of Mary and Joseph was the Christ: this cannot be so for the Christ was a Being of Spirit only and so Jesus, the son of Mary, was only a man: a teacher and prophet, the representative of the Christ on earth. For the Christ was a spirit only. Thus the crucifixion was not the death of the Christ. And it was for this reason that the followers of the Christ could meet and talk with him after the crucifixion. He who was the son of Mary and Joseph was a man, and he took a wife, and begot children, after the manner of his people and he being a Rabbi. But the Christ had no physical being: and it is the spiritual Christ whom we esteem and who will save us when we escape from the physical body that holds us imprisoned. For we are souls before we are bodies, and when our bodies are dead our joyful souls are made free. And for those souls who have truly learned the Way there is no need to be returned again to the flesh for they have conquered the desires of this world, and are made free. But some may choose to return to earthly life, in order to benefit the souls of others.

Now in the built Churches of Rome a line is drawn past which no woman may pass, being considered unclean by the priests: but we make no distinction as between men and woman since we see that women may be as much perfected as men. And women learn to heal and to instruct and to conduct both business and religious acts and therefore we honour woman

as much as we honour men who are perfected; for souls are of God and there can be no difference made between the soul of man and the soul of women. Women are gentler in many ways than men and can better tend the sick, the feeble and the young and helpless. Furthermore, they understand the Love of the Good God for the human souls that issue from God.

And in these latter days we see that there are more mysteries that we must learn, for as time passes we see that there are many things in which we saw but darkly in past days but now we see them in light. And the congress between men and women is in no ways as evil as we believed, for by the continuance of humankind we can see that more souls can learn of the things of the Good God.

Nevertheless, when we are released from the garment of flesh the soul rejoices, for it is free to return to its Source.

And also in these latter days we see that mankind has learned more of the Healing arts; and yet often the body is kept alive by means of machinery that prevents the escape of the soul. And many times this is against the wish of the soul, trapped within its robe of flesh, now defective. We believe that many things are done against the natural order which is ordained for mankind. Yet these things are done in love – and here is the mystery, for what is done in love cannot be evil yet still may not be the will of the Good God. And see, as yet we have not the answer to this mystery: and still we seek to heal, for the body suffers.

Now this Christ, who is our salvation and in whom is our hope and in whom we will make a good end, and in whom we trust to return to the Good God, is a Being of Spirit, and lives still in Spirit and in Truth; for the world has not yet recognised the Truth: that this was no man. And the Christ still shows the way in which to heal souls, and to heal the world. And we know that much good work is done in healing by many people who do not follow our way, but who are, in their own manner, perfected.

And these we honour, for the work is One, and still that work is that of defeating the wiles of the god of this world and for bringing the Light to souls in the whole world, that there may be perfect Love, Joy, and Peace. And we see that simple people do as we did in bygone days, and still go forth to tell, in simple words, how souls can learn perfection. We can see now that it is not only in our Path that Perfection lies – for the paths are many but the goal is one.'

Our own perception of what Catharism was and is:

The Cathar religion was and is a simple one: with very few rituals, no elaborate robes; meetings were held in any suitable place: outside among the trees, or in any room that could be made clean. They did not celebrate Mass, for they considered the eating of flesh and the drinking of blood both barbarous and cannibalistic, and extremely unholy. In fact the greatest sacrilege was to 'eat and drink god'.

The Cathars, who called them selves the 'Good Christians', were honourable, fair minded, hard working and caring men and women, who tried their best to live good and innocent lives and to help the people around them.

Their belief was that there were two, balancing, forces which operated in the world: that of the Good God, a spiritual being, and the source of all Love and all souls; and the other, lesser god – the god of the earth world - who strove to ensnare souls. This dualist doctrine was close to the Gnosticism of the Middle East.

The Cathars never took oaths, yet always kept their word; nor did they use bad language, but they spoke the tongue of the man in the street, rather than Latin, which was understood by very few, and they were truthful. They were frequently healers, herbalists, surgeons and bone setters, and cared for the sick and injured. They were sober, and yet were able to take innocent pleasure in the merry-making of the people around them, at harvest and other festive occasions. They were perhaps the first religiously motivated vegetarians, although they did eat fish, and they drank the wine of their country, but never to inebriation.

There was nothing cold or negative about the Perfecti, they were merry and loving, but strictly celibate. When they come to speak with us, they often make jokes so we feel that they were by no means 'stuffy' or 'holier than thou'. This religion is an ideal pathway for the twenty first century seeker after Truth and Light.

Consolamentum was almost the only rite of the Church of the Good Christians, who were also known as Cathars.

This rite was usually offered to Believers who were close to their physical death because the promises made in the Consolamentum are hard to keep, and should not be made unless the intention is, indeed, to keep them faithfully. Only men and women who had been married and whose partners in marriage consented to their partner taking these vows, would be 'consoled' when they were not about to die.

It was very rare for young, unmarried, persons to become 'Perfects'.

A.deG. & LS..

10 - Received Writing: What the Cathers have learned since the 13th Century.

'We have learned that there are two sides to every coin, and thus it is with our belief. We worship and obey the Good God, but we are aware of Asmodeus the god of this world from whose rule we attempt to escape.

We have also learned that the god of this world will always seek to entrap us and try to steal our souls away from the Good God to whom, in truth, they belong. And thus whenever a human child is born another soul is entrapped in that new body and must suffer the sadness of this world's pain, and attempt to be free of the god of this world. It is for this reason that we try to refrain from raising more children than we need to raise, seeing their souls will be imprisoned in their human bodies and may fall prey to the wiles of the evil god who makes this world and Its pitfalls.

But we know that if we abstain from all things that are tainted by procreation we are nearer to the light of the Good God.

It is for this reason, too, that we go about to heal and teach and to give a good example to our fellow men, because in that service we praise and serve God.

In the days when we first heard of this belief and were brought by reason of it from the way of the Roman Church, there were no preachers and no priests and there was no one in authority. And this was well, since no man or woman was set up above any other; yet in time we found that this was not practical. We are plain and practical folk who live in a hard land, and we need some organization. We therefore made shift to find some of those who were the most learned and the wisest, and more important yet, those who could most movingly speak to the people and could most tenderly care for them; and those we elected as bishops in our Church: but you must understand that our bishops are not as are the bishops of the Pope in Rome in that those bishops have great lands and high estates and are very often worldly men. But our bishops are truly shepherds unto their flocks, and they have no wealth to use for their own affairs nor do they have palaces of stone and embroidered garments or great estates, but are as we all are, except that they have greater gifts to offer.

Our bishops go forth mostly on foot and they take with them one whom they train to succeed them, in case they should die, or should be made to die, for many hands are turned against us. These successors are chosen for the gifts which the Good God has given them and they are taught how best to employ those gifts by travelling with their bishop and learning from his words and deeds, and from conversing with him.

We have no priests, but we have elders which have long learned our Beliefs and can instruct others. Now, these elders are called "Perfecti and the women who are wise are called likewise Perfectae, which is to say that they too have been perfected in the knowledge of our Belief and can offer the sacrament of 'Consolamentum,' which we use for praising the Good God and the care of men and women. Now,we have told of the way in which we initiate a Perfecti, and this is a simple and a beautiful rite, and is nothing like to the corrupted rituals of the Church of Rome.

As well as the bishops and the perfected ones, we have many who are 'believers' and these have not yet accepted Consolamentum, neither have they asked for it, yet still they believe, and still their hearts and minds and their souls are with us. And these 'croyants', when they know that their time ihas come that they must leave the life of this world, usually take the Consolamentum and end their days as perfected ones. These Believers will walk for many miles by difficult ways and in harsh conditions so that they may pray together, or may hear the words of a bishop or a Perfecti.

And we gather together in fields or in clearings in the forest for we do not wish to build, spending much money and much time, as do those of Rome. Yet there are some small churches and chapels which account themselves of our Belief, but they are few.

The whole of our teaching is love, simplicity and purity – and mirth, for we laugh at no man and at no woman, yet we laugh with them. Although our bishops and our parfaits are seemly and grave, and read deeply in many books and scrolls, and have argued and discussed each point of our belief, yet they are merry, and they do not show a sad face to the people, for that would discourage the people and then maybe they would be forever lost

Now the Call to serve the Good God , maker of all things comes in many ways: some care for the sick, some care for the small treasure that belongs to our Church: this is indeed small and is mostly books, but we are in necessity to buy needful certain things, so that it is important that we have men of business amongst us. And we have men and women who serve as scribes and copyists, for we have obtained writings on many subjects and must copy and pass on this knowledge, so that this is no longer hidden from the children of God.

For in the Church of Rome all the rites and prayers are recited in a foreign tongue unknown to those who listen. And indeed it is often unknown by those who say the prayers and conduct the rites for they learn by rote and speak what their memory tells them or what, if they can read, they see before them, but not what they understand in their heart. This is then a lie: their prayers are lies for they know nothing of what they read or recite, for all they may be men of love and care and peace: for see, you cannot feed children with flour only but must mix it and bake it into bread, and then they may eat of it; but that priest who does not understand what he says offers only flour and water, unsalted, unleavened and unbaked. How then can he, however much love is in his heart, feed his children thus?

Now our writings and our copying of other writings, from which we have gained knowledge of many things, are our most prized treasure for each one is a casket of gems for the soul. Thus those who inscribe the writings of others and who note and relate the teachings of our Perfecti are our especial workers for it is not an easy thing to write and often we must do so in hiding where there is but little comfort for the body: yet there come forward good men and women, Perfecti, who offer to do this work. And so that our works may be known and our teachings kept before the eyes of men, we send these writings out into the world so that they may come to every country in the language of that country; but there are some tongues that we do not have, and for these only we construe in Latin for there is always one who understands the Latin tongue.

The lords of our country being kindly and well disposed to our teachings have put at our disposal not only places of privacy where we may write, but have also made gifts of parchment and ink so that we are provided with materials. And the lords, when they can read and write (and many there are who cannot) peruse our teachings in our books and where-so-ever they cannot read we will with great joy read to them that which we have written, for we neither speak nor write evil things, but only those things that are good and true and meet and right to do and to read.

It has pleased the Good God to send us men of great intellect to work with us – but these men never sign their works for that would be sure to invite the soldiers of the Roman church to descend upon us.

There is a lady and she is a Lady of great wealth and beauty of soul and of goodness, and her soul is pure; and she is now widowed and a dowager. And this good lady conveys away books to places where they are needed, and she makes them secure, for they are hidden in water skins and loaded onto the mules and donkeys which take the produce of her fields and vineyards to other parts. I may not say her name but I can say that she lives between Carcassonne and Foix.

And see! We do not celebrate the Mass as do the Romans who claim that bread and wine are transubstantiated into the flesh and blood of Jesus. For in our eyes this is the last barbarity – to eat a man: still more to eat one who is by some regarded as a god. We gather together to share a meal, and we break bread and take wine together, and this is our way. And when one is dying, then comes one of the Perfectii to offer the Consolamentum; but this is not done unless the person is certain to die, for the healing Love of God will work in many ways, so that the person may recover and then repent them that they took the Consolamentum.'

On The Consolamentum

'We stand, clockwise,
a candle burning:
not all of us are wise
to know the turning.
We wander back in time
To such a softer clime,
Our spirits burning –
Burning! The candle
is our minds, not wise,
but always daring
to seek for Truth amongst
the hidden learning.
We move, clockwise:
not all of us are wise
to know the saying –
to wander down the years,
remember, praying,
in caves where candles burn,
in fields where prayers turn –
while we are burning.'

Writing found 27/01/2003.Repudiation of the negativity of
Catharism

'Men have declared, in concert, that there are naught but
negatives in our Truth; but see I will show you that our beliefs
and knowledge is as positive as that greater 'heresy' – the
heresy of Rome.
For we saw that the Good God made all souls, and before
anything else existed there was God and of Himself did God
create all the worlds which He required for His purposes. And
the Angels and Archangels he made, before he made souls for
mankind. Then one of the bright angels, full of light, and
named Lucifer, which is 'light bearer' challenged God,
demanding that as he was part of God and created from God
he should be as great as God. But this could not be, seeing
that he was but a small portion of God. But, in wisdom, God
gave to him any soul that he might ensnare from God.
For God knew that He had Himself put wisdom into the souls
that He had made for mankind, so that the souls would know
light from dark, and would know right from wrong and those
who chose light and right would not be lost to Lucifer that
proud one, also called Asmodeus – god of this world.
And God had caused the world to be made according to His
plan. He put into the world all manner of things that are
needful for life but the Good God enjoined the souls He made
for mankind not to be wasteful and luxurious and not to use
to excess those things that He had provided. And it is for this
that we take no life, no, not even for food.
We live as simply ,and dress as is decently appropriate, for
that place in which we live for climate and for modesty,
covering ourselves with good garments well made of good
cloth but not rich; and we eat the fruits of the earth as given

to us by God, for the plants that grow provide for our needs. Herbs there are in plenty to heal and to comfort us when sick or injured and all manner of things may be made from those plants both to eat and to drink and to heal and to serve.

Then, when the Good God saw that His rebellious angel, into whose hands He had placed the earth, was gaining more power over the souls by making them greedy, lustful, drunken and luxurious, so then He sent messengers to show the souls of mankind where their faults lay.

And one of those messengers was Jesus whose name we know from the book of John, who as the most beloved follower of Jesus and a holy man.

Now there came a time when the followers of this man Jesus put the messenger before God and called Jesus 'Lord' and made him to be a god: but this he could not be, seeing that he was a man born of a woman whose name was Maria and that he had a father, too, a man of this world.

Then there came those who would have us believe, many tales of this messenger, Jesus (whose name in his own tongue was Yeshua) for though he was endued with great powers yet he could not be a god, since God had made his soul as for every member of mankind. At first all was well and men followed the teachings of the messenger; but gradually those who were in command of the works of this messenger decided that he should be glorified so that they should bask in his glory and they preached that only to believe in him was surely to be saved from everlasting life over and over again, and from everlasting fire and torment. And thus they made him into a god.

When wiser men said that this could not be, the followers, corrupted by the power that they had assumed for themselves, began in vanity to persecute those honest souls.

For our whole belief is this, that the messenger of God came to show us how to live a simple life in love and peace with all life, and that we should care for each other as brothers and sisters and should care for the life of all that lives on the earth that the Good God placed here to dwell and that we should sustain the well-being of the world.

Nor should we lift hands in anger, but seek peace. Where ever there is suffering from disease, there it is that we should seek to alleviate it by the influx of the Spirit of the Loving God, through our souls, to those who suffer. And we should not benefit from the mischance of anyone; nor should we engage in unclean acts. And we believe that when we have lived here for a certain time in a human body and when that body fails us then we must seek another and another, until we have learned the Perfect Love, Tolerance, and Wisdom, which will reunite us with the Good God: for sparks of the Spirit of God we are, and so we remain.

Now in time the priests who would take unto themselves all power and stand between God and us percieved that what which we preached and lived was good and just; and being jealous, they attacked our precepts of common sense and common purpose. So they told lies about our life; they made accusations against us because we took no part in vice, usury, and violence; and they were abashed and had no answers for our good lives. And so they persecuted us and said that our beliefs were of negatives – but these men could not know the beauty of communing with God through the natural landscape rather than in buildings; they could not know how sweet was the taste of honestly grown and harvested foods, and the fresh water of springs provided by God; nor yet the happiness of wearing simple garments, made with love.

Nor could they understand that we saw no value in a cross,

symbol of torture and shame, but there is much value in a loaf of bread shared with like-minded ones, or a cup of wine shared by all alike and a blessing said on all those who would be blessed.

They had fallen into the snares of the god of this world and wished only for luxurious food and many possessions, and rich clothing and furnishings. And they knew no longer how sweet is the sound of praise, sung in the open air as God ordained. And they placed much worth in old stories and tales that were untrue and ridiculous, and so they brow-beat and misled the simple folk whom they entranced to follow them.'

Received Writing, February, 2004, (but written prior to that date) and intended for Llyn, (Guillielm) from the Cathar Bishop, Bertrand Marty:

'My beloved Eldest Son, I wish you to know why we did not feel it necessary that you should toil all the way up to the summit and to the ruined castle of Montsegur. You must understand Guillielm that the walls that stand today, crowning the mountain, are not the walls that were where we all lived and worked and prayed for so many weary months. Now, when the castle capitulated at our request and all was finished, the men of Simon de Montfort and his cronies dismantled the strong mountain castle – every stone.

What you see today is not the place where we, the good Christians, resided. The homes and the places of work of the Bons Chretiens were broken down and demolished. The castle that you see today is all that remains of that built by the French King for his personal glorification – why then should you struggle to reach the place?

Thus we arranged for the snow to prevent you and so we in

this forced you and your friend, who is ever foolishly inclined to do more than she can well, manage, to stand in the field. We showed you where the burning took place.

The Monument was placed much later where the ashes were decently interred. And there, where you both perished of the body, we have given you Consolamentum, both then, in those days, and now in these days. So now you must again go forth to spread our truth to those who will hear. '

Received Writing 27/5/2004.

'It did not matter whether it was the Lord's castle or his servant's cottage, so the room was clean and seemly; if there was no safe room, we met in woodlands and fields; there would we meet with one candle alight on a white cloth, white as it could be laundered, and spread on a table or if there was no table then upon any piece of furniture or a large basket up-turned. On the cloth was also placed the testament of John the Apostle, he whom The Master Jesus best loved.

Then we would gather together, all the men to one side and all the women to the other.

They stood there in no order - master and man, lady and maid, side by side, shoulder to shoulder for with the Good God there is no rank or station in life but only service and learning, healing and teaching, working and preaching. And all this was in order to save souls.

And to this end we met then and to that end we meet now. For the work is the same as well you know, and it has been, all down the steppes of Time! For if men and women will but live well, doing good and not committing foolishness, they can find a way out of the cycle of fleshly incarnation and become pure spirit. Then they may rejoin the Source and be at one again with the Good God. But this is an estate given to very few, for the way is hard and the world tempts so many away from their desired path.

We tried then to help men and women to hear our Way: never to curse or to blaspheme, never to promise what they could not perform, never to steal, never to lie, never to betray another's words or life and not to fear death, in whatsoever form it might come. For death is as nothing compared to the hurt a soul might receive from the scars of the world.

And as we tried diligently to lead the people along the paths of righteousness, so also we worked amongst them in their everyday lives: we spun thread, wove cloth, made clothes and shoes, worked with wood and in clay, and trod the grape and gathered the olive. We dug and scythed and sang with them.

In these ways we gained the trust and love of the people, for we imposed no taxes and kept no mistresses and we never owed debts to anyone: nor did we over-eat or become drunk. And because we led abstemious, worthwhile lives and were honest and humble and good neighbours, we won the respect of men and women in our Country.

And because we had been schooled in medicine and the Healing Arts, they brought their sick to us – and where these could not come to us, we went to them. And where we could, we made them whole, and where we could do nothing but alleviate suffering that we did, and gave the Consolamentum, the Consolation of our Holy Way, to those who could not recover their health and whose time had come to leave the flesh.

We kept no mistresses or lovers; and we married no wives and no husbands: we had no time and no need for any such partners.

Yet we were courteous to all womenfolk, and they stood with

us at our meetings, at whatever age and in whatever station in life, for their souls too are the children of the Good God. And the people saw that our honest lives were pure, although we honoured womanhood.

We drank what we needed, and no more! We drank the wine of the countryside and water from springs and wells.

And so fresh were our palates that we could say with certainty from which well the water we drank had been drawn.

We worked hard enough to pay our way in life. And we owed no money to anyone. So people saw that we were chaste, sober, industrious, and solvent.

We ate no meat but took a little fish, bread, vegetables and fruit. So that it was seen that we were not gluttons.

The people saw the priests of the Roman Church - that they ate and drank to excess, that they had their doxies and that they gambled, that they were idle and their Latin so poor that no wise man could understand when they said Mass or any other of the sacraments of their Church.

They also exacted monies from the people, whether the people could afford those taxes or not

So the people compared these idle priests to us and to others of our persuasion and calling: and they saw that we were better men than the priests. They watched our women as they diligently went about their duties with the sick and the injured and worked in their own households and they saw that our women lived more harmoniously and chastely than did the nuns of the Roman Church.

Therefore the people loved us, both men and women and called us the 'Good Men' and the 'Good Women'. And they came to us for help and guidance and it was both our privilege and our delight to help them, to teach them and tell them how the world truly is...'.

(this is where the script trails off into unreadable scribble; obviously
I was too deeply asleep to control the pen. Ade G.)

Automatic Writing found on 17/7/2001:

'And you, Guillielm, will recall the work which you
accomplished, both in recording our Laws and our ritual and
also in recording the happenings of those times and the
doings of great men as well as the peasants, so that in future
time men would know of what we did. Know that your work is
still preserved both in Spain and Irelaunde where there was
no dissension between us and the Church of Rome, for the
Irelaundaises had ever their own way of following the Lord.
Know too that to this day the rites and the work which you do
is the continuance of that work which you did in our Country.
You work in a different tongue but with the same heart.*

Your work now is to reconcile the minds, hearts of men and
women who suffer to their souls, and the work that they must
do in order that they may live to the best of this world, and
ready to be at last removed from the flesh and joined once
more to the Good God whose children they are. So you see
the rites that now you follow and the ways in which you call
upon the Good God are of no significant difference to the work
which you did so long ago in our land of sunshine and flowers.
You have lived and learned many times and each life has
shown you more of the hearts of men. Now you have studied
their minds also, for the two do not always agree! So soon you
will be even wiser. And you will be able soon to see that cord
of silver that joins all men to their souls and that joins all souls
to the Creator. But this you know. How much more proof is it
needful for me to give you? Know you not that the friend who
laid down the rites that you once practised was also of our

number?

He may not have recalled it in his most recent life, and thus he called on many gods, in order to call on the One. Yet he knew: and he knew too our abilities to withdraw from the body in necessity. So he too knew of rebirth and the seeking of that which he called the 'grail' was the truth that we carried in our hearts and in our ways. The time is seamless betwixt now and then.

He wrote as he thought, thinking as he remembered. His words were different but yet they were same and sprang from the same Source. You still walk in your ancient footsteps.

For I tell you that from your earliest recall, before Crete, through Egypt, through the Bon Hommes and through all other times, your path has been the same; your faith has not wavered and your flame has not burnt itself out.

Know too that we have work still for you to do, and that you will accomplish, and we will not allow your capability for accomplishing it to be removed from you – that which you love will go on and prosper.
But you will never be satisfied and content, for such is the nature of your questing soul. While others find their peace with ease, you will find yours always in struggle – it is your nature, so be it and be blessed in that knowledge.
Yet be gentle with your own mind, as you are with others, for you also are a child of the Good God, however small a spark you consider yourself.
And recall, that from the Nations of your father comes wisdom also, and that you have learned and will learn. For your grandmother has told you that in the fall of the year 2000 you would find her, and she would be with you to help and

preserve you: and recall now, she was. For in that time much was added to you both in the material world and in the spiritual world and in the world of effort and struggle which you encountered. Be not afraid, for the Right and the Light will overcome wrong and darkness and all those with whom you have lived in the world of flesh will gather to your aid from the realms of Spirit of the One Good God. Trust and pray. Trust and pray.

This woman whom I have made my amanuensis has been unable to write to my dictation. But now she is now enabled once more and there will be more information, more teaching and more communication. You will find the hollow rock that you have seen in dreams: it will be changed but you will know it again.

Be strong for the experience will be hard to bear and your recall will make your head spin and your heart tighten. But all is at peace now and the suffering is past. See all things distantly and know that you are made anew and need suffer no more: think only of the sweet and innocent life that you then led, though well versed in the world's ways, and see and rejoice. Do not see and weep. The ashes are blown away, the blood is washed away. The price was paid then and today's Seeing is free from sorrow.

You will meet others there whom you will know in places where you have not met them before. And some who were there and who you do not recall will also present themselves and you will know them. Be uplifted, for see! All is well – THEY LIVE!

And they live as themselves as do you. Be happy.

You have paid for your journey in this time by your good grace in that time.

Accept the gift of the Good God: your soul is safe. Amen'.

*A Cathar script is kept in a library in Dublin.
A Received Writing:

'Sometimes the people were unwilling to accept money from us, so then we gave them little gifts – whatever we had that we could spare: a book, if we had two, one of our knives or shoes that we had made in our idle moments.
Years later I discovered that, when we had eaten with them, our hosts would take morsels of bread that we had left uneaten and keep them for use when anyone was sick: they called these morsels 'holy bread' and thought that because we had said a Grace over our food before we ate, it would have properties that would confer renewed health! They used it too, if someone was about to die and there was no Perfecti available to offer Consolamentum. Our life was simple, honest, abstinent and fun: we were loved wherever we went and welcomed in most of the Courts and noble houses of the lands where we lived. The aristocrats of Occitania were not only Cathars or friendly to us, but also civilised, cultivated and educated people who enjoyed discussing art, music and poetry and often philosophy, mathematics and science too.
They were glad of our skills as scholars and often asked advice on political matters – we travelled and mixed with many people in many places so that we had a good understanding of what was happening everywhere. Thus we were welcomed at every level of society.'

11 - Received Writing: About the choice of workers.

For our travelling teachers we chose strong and sturdy, well grounded men and women, who knew the land and the People well: those who knew the tongue, the habits and the particular dishes of the neighbourhood. For such as these knew the most secret needs of the People, their hopes and fears, even whether they had the means to pay the taxes imposed by their lords. Such as these could know the people and be known by them, be trusted and respected.

Thus those we had chosen to go forth were specially prepared for their task. And the first preparation was that they should know all the deep truths of our Way and Belief.

Therefore it was of great importance that they were all capable of reading and of writing; so that they could offer all help. They could cast up numbers and multiply and subtract numbers, this being of good use to simple folk when tax-time came and their rents were due. And so that our brothers and sisters could maintain themselves we ensured that they had trades also.

The women knew how to card, to spin and weave and to sew. They were taught receipts for simples, as were the men, and they learned such simple surgery as a woman might accomplish: which is to say that which their hands were strong enough to perform, for bones are hard to saw into and such things as amputations must be done exceedingly quickly, else the patient may die, so that men were better for such work; but our women had other duties in healing, and they used those ways of healing as were dictated to us from heaven. Women were nimble fingered too, and could close up wounds and make poultices and syrups. We ensured also that they knew how to care for animals so that they were useful to the farmers and drovers whom they met along their way.

We taught our men-folk farming skills, as well as writing, and they learned the healing arts, like their sisters, but so that they might always get their bread they learned also a trade – as blacksmithing or leather-work or baking or shoemaking.

Many of our men were good seams-men and they could sew as well as any woman and in the case of very heavy stuffs they sewed more easily than women could, and some learned the trade of weaving and embroidery or the craft of wood-working.

In these ways we ensured that our brothers and sisters were not a burden to the communities in which they found themselves, for they brought much to the people and took nothing from them but that which was paid for and for this reason they were called 'bons hommes' and 'bonnes femmes' because they took nothing but gave much.

And on all these children of light we laid other burdens also: one of these being that they had to prove that they could not only speak with the people, but also to them. We showed them how to make their voices great so that every soul in the crowd could hear them.

We showed them how to speak with folk in honest mirth, making sport for them, for though we ate no meat we did not live lives of abstention from laughter and our mirth was great and our souls, unencumbered by earthly things, were blithe. And we showed them how to teach easily and to make plain their beliefs and the Way of Light.

 And we showed them how to live, and how to help other people to live, so that the people could believe, if they wished, that which we believed, so that they might be at last be safe having been consoled and committed in true belief.

Yet never did we seek to impose our will upon others by force, for we only showed what our faith was and that they might choose it if they would.

And these things were taught to our men and women so that they might go out into the fields and forests and into the towns and villages to live with the people, helping them and serving them and teaching them also.

This we did for a Light to lighten the darkness in which many lived, and to comfort them.

For the work that they had to do we not only trained their bodies and minds, but we also provided the tools of the trades that they had learned, and clothing useful to them in the world.

For we kept no garments apart, as did the religious of the Church of Rome, but our women went modestly garbed, as did our men, in good stuff gowns and cloaks with hoods to them and stout shoes for winter and stockings too for the cold; for although our country is warm yet in the mountains it is cold and there comes snow and a chill wind.

So we sent them forth by two and by two to live in the world, and not shut away in cloisters but living usefully in the bosom of the people, earning their keep and paying their way and helping their brothers and sisters. For are we not all one family? And is not this a Holy Family?

And each of our wayfarers carried a few coins in their purse, and a Book of St John, for it was by that Holy Disciple that the Light came to be known in this world, teaching us, the children of Light, to seek that Light again!

With this book we taught our travelling people all that they needed to do and to say to heal souls, whether those souls were to stay in bodies or whether they were to leave their earthen bodies to seek another, newer one.

So we taught the all Bons Hommes and the Bonnes Femmes

to minister to souls and counsel them at the end of that earth journey so that they could come again, as new lives in the Light.

Then on an auspicious day, a good-seeming day, for we were not superstitious as are the unlearned.

We called them all together and bid them choose a partner for the road for we sent them out and two together, or sometimes three – a man and a woman, or a woman and two men. And we made sure that they were of different ages, so that wherever they went they could understand the needs of all ages and conditions of people, young and old, rich and poor alike.

And we confirmed them in the True belief laying the Holy Book on each head bowed, and seeing as each one gave Consolamentum to their partners, so that we could see that this was well done.

Yet not all the Rite was used since these were not dying, but that part that pertains to death was omitted.

And after that we gathered together at the supper board and broke bread together and passed the Cup one to the other. And we were all very merry together and blessed each other and the Work we were to do for the Light.

And next day early after breaking their fast, these set off in all directions into the world to fill it with Light. For we lived in the Light and the Light lived in us and so we became the Light: the Light of the World of the Good God we brought so that all people could see it and some would follow.

And though our Way is a humble Way, yet it is a Way of Truth and Light.

We taught the people that Jesus was a Child of Light and the Christ Spirit and we told them the plain Truth and not the lies that others had added to the Truth for that Story was simple and needed no embellishment.

We showed them how to live cleanly and simply but happily and to live in the Light of the Good God, and how to avoid the snares of the god of this world who longs for the souls of men and women which he thinks will make him great.

But that is foolishness for see, a rich man adds many coins to his treasure chest but they cannot buy him the True Light nor can he by rubbing two coins together make fire or water nor may he eat the coins for his hunger but only use them to buy food; and if there is no food to buy then he must starve like poor men starve, however rich he may become.

So does Asmodeus, god of this world, seek to feed on the coinage of the Good God: which is human souls.

And it was for the avoidance of Asmodeus and his snare that we went forth to the people that they might learn and save their souls. So it was that the story of the Bons Hommes and the Bonnes Femmes in their dark blue mantles was borne all over our lands and even into other lands, just as it had come to us from those who lived afar off and ever that Living afar off was told of and prophesied in the Book of John the Beloved one: for he writes of the Light coming to lighten the gentiles.

When they came to a place where the trade they had learned was needed and where the people were willing that they should dwell, our Heralds of Light stopped and found lodging and soon began their work with the people.

And as our Way is a Way of Light, so were we loved by the people who soon began to follow all our counsels and to live iin much harmony with us and with each other, and with the Good God. And this was how we accomplished our work.

These whom we sent forth to live amongst the people were pledged to bring the Truth to them, for the Church of Rome willing to subdue all souls to itself, had long sought to frighten these same souls into salvation. So they preached a Gospel not so much of redemption as of condemnation, teaching the people that if they did not follow the teachings of the Roman Church they would burn in Hell for all eternity, ever subjected to torments.

Now this was not that message of Love and salvation that was given to mankind when Mary brought forth her son into this world, for that son taught salvation by Love.

So we went forth to teach the people this simple Truth that we knew, that we must come into this world and that we must stay here, until we have learned enough to see that we may go forward into the Light of God.

And that while we are in this world, we may learn how tour souls may progress from always returning to this world.

We may find this learning by the way in which we live our lives; and in this way shall we find peace.

For look, Peace comes into the hearts of people at one with themselves, those with whom they share Life, and with God: not the god of this world but the Good God, Creator of all things.

To this end we showed people how to live their lives in quiet and peace, one with another: that they draw no blood save for a medical reason, to take no life, to live chastely, to barter fairly and live honestly, to bear witness always to the truth and to live cleanly and in peace with all the world.

So we showed them how they could better themselves and avoid yet more returns to this world so that their souls need not further hunt for new bodies but could accept Consolamentum and move into the nearer Presence of the Good God.

But the priests of Rome hated us because we spoke the truth, because we did not accept bribes, and because people saw that we were honest men and women, merciful, chaste and honest and of good repute. Therefore, being unable to buy our silence, the priests of Rome sought to destroy us. And they told very frightful stories to certain rich lords who they knew to be in a state of sinfulness: they promised these men that their sins would be expunged if they would but hunt out the 'Bons Hommes' and 'Bonnes Femmes' when they could find them and bring them to "justice".

So then these nobles and knights, fearing the might of Rome and the wrath of the Pope of Rome, began to seek out any who were pledged to our Belief.

But those people who loved us and who knew of the good lives that we led, and of all our good offices to them, would never in any wise give us up to those men, nor say which were our houses. Furthermore, most of the lords of that land in which we dwelt were themselves Croyants - believers in our Faith and followers of our Path - along with us.

And where a lord was not of our Belief it was most like that his lady or his mother or his sister was, thus were we safe for many years following quietly the Path that we had chosen.

Yet I would tell you that we were not morose men, although we were peaceful for our life was joyous rather than gloomy and the Way that we followed was, and still is a Path of joy and of gladness, for we know that life does not cease at the grave's edge but that we continue to be in existence and that we may come again to this world and if we have learned enough we shall be reunited with our Good God at His Pleasure.

So we lived, simply, in good faith and with much joy and thus we should have continued in those lands until now, had it not been for the Might of Rome whose dark works May the Good God pardon!'

'We called ourselves 'Good Christians'; the people amongst whom we lived and worked called us 'les Bons Hommes' and 'les Bonnes Femmes' (the Good Men and the Good Women). The Roman Catholics chose to call us Albigensiens, after the town of Albi where they mistakenly thought we had our strongest following, or else 'Cathars' from the Greek word 'cathari' for 'pure ones' – and this was meant sarcastically, but because of our genuinely good, and well intentioned lives, the term has remained with us.

We believe that the universe was made and ruled by the Good God, the Force of Good but that there is also a Force of Evil which we called Asmodeus – the god of this world, a fallen angel who tries to imprison souls. We believed and do believe, that Jesus was a great and good Teacher, who carried the 'Christ Spirit', but that he was not God.

We do not believe in the 'virgin birth' or the resurrection of the physical body and we looked, and look still, upon the crucifix as a symbol of oppression, torture and death.

We believed, and still believe, that souls must work for their salvation by living decent lives – no one can save their soul when their only gesture towards 'goodness' is to say they believe in someone else's death on their behalf: it is not enough to lay all their sins at the door of one man – Jesus, who carried the Christ Spirit – and imagine that this would somehow purchase their own salvation.

We knew that we had to work hard at improving ourselves and that we may have to return to human bodies many times before we are fit to rejoin the Good God.

'Cathars' did not celebrate Mass (Holy Communion) in the way that the Roman Catholics and some other Christians do, for that we thought it nothing short of barbarous to imagine eating human flesh and drinking human blood – even more revolting to us is the thought of eating and drinking God.

Imagine what becomes of whatever we eat and drink – for the cesspit is no place for God!

We did, however, share a common meal, at the start of which wine and bread were blessed and shared by all who were present as a token of friendship and of family – much like to a Jewish Sabbath meal.

We did not have priests and we did not pay the tribute money to the Pope.

We spoke to the people in their own language, which they understood, instead of the Latin used by the Roman priests, which was a mystery to the unlearned. Thus the Roman Catholic hierarchy hated and feared us. The majority of the nobles of land of the Langue d'Oc, from the sea to the Pyrenees, and to the other mountains, were either Cathars themselves, or their families were Cathars or they were at the least sympathetic to our beliefs.

The land where we dwelt was vast and rich and as the English Crown held much land in Anjou, Aquitaine, Gascony, Normandy and elsewhere, and with our land being a collection of independent and separate states, prosperous, and allied to Aragon and Catalonia, it became inevitable that the French king would wish to add our land to his own small domain.

His position, like his treasury was weak, his actual lands were small. Thus that the ruling Houses of our land were either Cathar or friendly to the Cathars, and therefore 'heretical', the French King and the Pope made an excuse to conspire to eject our local lords, to confiscate their lands and to burn as many of us as they could catch.

They caught many hundreds.

This atrocity was called a crusade; it was always about riches and land, for none of these 'nobles', named 'crusaders', were pious men.

Our chief scripture was the Gospel of St. John, without a copy of which we never stirred.

The concept of Light - the Light of the World - was the central pillar of our view of the Good God, the Source of all Light and all Life.

We were strictly vegetarian and those who became 'perfected' refrained from sexual connections.

We valued women as highly as men and our women were able to take their places in our meetings – whereas in the Roman Catholic Churches a line was drawn at the back of the building and women were not allowed to cross that line – and yet their priests hailed the 'virgin' Mary, the mother of Jesus, as the 'Mother of God'!

Since we had no built churches we had no such lines and because we knew that Jesus was a man and his mother had conceived in the usual way, and we believed that women had as much right to God as men had.

Our Perfecti did not have the status of priests and if they disobeyed the rules, then they had to go back, start their training again and seek perfection once more just as did the ordinary local people.

The 'Perfecti' were always ready to help with the work of the people wherever they happened to be, whether in the countryside with the harvesting or the sowing or with weaving or leather work in towns and villages.

We were always on hand to help in any way that we could, reading or writing letters for the illiterate, making peace between people who had fallen out with each other, and offering the Consolamentum to those who requested it

We were abstinent in every way and we did not expect the people to pay for us for we kept ourselves by working and although we were often offered gifts by those who could afford to do so we never asked for anything.

This was in such stark contrast to the Roman priests who demanded tithes and took whatever they wanted and often led lazy and or dissolute lives, that the people loved us and preferred to look to the Good Christians for their examples, seeing that we lived lives that far more closely resembling that of Jesus, than did the Roman priests.

Thus they turned to us for spiritual counsel and comfort. Sadly,this further annoyed both the King of France and the Bishop of Rome!Rome.

In addition to refraining from meat and dairy products we also fasted on at least one day a week and at certain times of the year we fasted more.

There were universities which we set up, where scholars from Christianity, Judaism and Islam studied together and shared their knowledge. This was of great assistance, as the Jews and Muslims were adept in medicine and surgery and we could learn much.

We also had access via our Muslim colleagues to many ancient writings. Thus it was that we could read scriptures of the early Christian Church that were now forbidden to other Christians to read or to copy out.

Our Jewish colleagues also told us of their beliefs and regulations for health for all knowledge and wisdom was welcomed by us and we held no man's religious views against him so long as he lived a good life and was decent and honourable.

In time we had both colleges and hospitals, where study and care were free for those who required them.

For these reasons, too, the people loved us but the Roman Catholic hierarchy hated us.

All the 'Perfecti' went about the countryside preaching and teaching to save souls and we went about in twos, for in that way we might remind each other to say the great prayer before we ate or drank and to behave well - for we well knew that we were but ordinary men and women.

We made a promise to the Good God never to swear any oaths, cheat or lie, and that we would read the Holy Book.

Because they always saw two Cathar men walking together, with no women present the priests of Rome assumed, else they pretended to assume, that we practised homosexual acts, for they could not understand how men who were not priests could be celibate: but Perfects did undertake celibacy, which was why they were normally chosen from men and women who had been married and were now prepared to become celibate and whose partners were in accord. We found life joyous – we laughed much and life was a happy adventure.

As we walked along – for we had no horses and ivery few personal possessions with which we could concern ourselves we found much to discuss and debate and to be gratefully joyful for. When we were in need, we worked at any job that was available, teaching any who wished to know of the Faith, as we worked. Sometimes it was farming, gathering in the harvest, or weaving, or any craft to which we might turn our hands; and we were happy and safe, until all things changed, and strangers came amongst us.'

Writings.1/10/2001

And it has been falsely rumoured that the Perfected Ones used strange rites, that they were guilty of lechery and greed – but these are false tales made by corrupt priests of Rome, which were themselves guilty. For they did not study the way, and nor did they help the people. Rather did they use the common people, extorting from them both goods and, where they had any, money. And these so-called priests made free also with the women who were in their care, deflowering them, and using them lewdly. And they ate and drank immoderately and wore garments unsuitable to holy men.But the Perfected were moderate in all things, eating no unclean thing, taking only diluted wine, and mostly water, and rejecting sexual contact. But their Way of Perfection was not understood by the Roman priests, who, therefore told these false stories; but the common people of the villages, fields, mountains and markets knew the goof life of the Perfects, that these were those to whom they could turn for healing in sickness, comfort in adversity, light in dark and troubled times, and Holy Peace at their passing.

For all our philosophy was of Love: Love Divine of the Good God for the souls, his children, and of these children for the Good God. Yet many men and women were overcome by the wiles of Asmodeus, and did not follow our way, but fell by the wayside. And these will now be re-born, yet again, to service in a new garment of flesh, until they come at last to see the Truth of the Good God whose children they are. These, then, had no love in their lives, but only lust, gluttony and avarice and had no charity, nor any knowledge of the Truth of the Love of the Good God. Yet in time even these will learn, whether by the teaching of other, more Perfected souls, or from their own experiences in the many lives. For the Good God wastes no seeds. And the seeds of our life are the creations of the Good God, for our true lives reside in our souls, who are the children of the Good God, so that righteousness must at last conquer vice and depravity.Yet those who have knowledge do not follow the paths of depravity, eschewing vice and corruption, they eat not animals' flesh, nor do they consort in sexual intercourse unless only when they are not yet perfected, and have not yet learned enough to know that this only makes more bodies for souls to use who know not truth. And yet those who are perfected do not look down on those who have not learned – nor do they judge them, for it is said that the |Good God alone has the right of judgement of the children, the souls that are seeds of God. And perfected souls will instruct, cure, and care for all other souls who ask and truly beseech for learning. And they will go forth, two by two, travelling wherever need is great; and as they go, not only do they teach Truth, but they serve by Healing and by helping in allwise those who they find in their path way. And by this service of love are they beloved of the people, who will hide and help the Perfected when there is need. And now in the world of men is great need of healing and helping and of Truth, more than ever in those times of the burning of our people's bodies. For man has outstretched himself and has challenged the laws of the universe and of the Good God; and in this there is no health but only harm. And so now is time for all Perfected souls to come to help and heal yet again, for that man will always do ill if he be not taught better. And now there are many souls living in fleshly bodies who are Perfected Ones but who come to teach and heal and to help. And so God bless you and may the Light That Shines In darkness be on you.

Found on 1/10/2001.
'And when at last came the final moment of life in the physical body, family, friends and the Perfectii gathered about the dying one, and gave their blessing by the laying on of hands to the soul that was setting forth in search of its rightful place.

It was prepared by Consolamentum for the change while still in the body of flesh which it wore as a garment for this brief life only.

And the empty body was taken and buried with care in some suitable place.

And if the soul returned again to the same place where it had previously lived in the flesh then that soul would know again all the places that it knew in life on earth, and where the previous garment of flesh had been placed.

Never the less, Perfected souls did not usually return to this world, except in spiritual form, for the Perfecti had found the Way and came only to instruct and comfort.

Know then, as you live in the flesh, and learn that those who have preceded you go with you, helping and instructing.

So it is that some whose ears and eyes are open may see the Perfecti who walk with them.

And many refer to these as 'guardian angels' but in truth the angels are as different to these souls as man is to the animals.

For the angels see the Good God and stand around the seat of God, awaiting the Holy Will.

And it has falsely been rumoured that the Perfected Ones used strange rites, and that they were guilty of lechery and greed: but these are false tales made by the corrupt priests of Rome and of these misdemeanours were they themselves guilty. They did not study the Way nor did they help the people. Rather did they use the common people, extorting from them both money and goods. These so-called priests made free with the women who were in their care, deflowering them and using them lewdly. And they ate and drank immoderately and wore garments unsuitable to holy men.

These then had no love in their hearts but only lust, gluttony and avarice and had no charity, nor any knowledge of the truth of the love of God.

Yet, in time, even these will learn Truth whether by the teachings of other, more Perfected souls, or from their own experiences in their many lives.

The Perfecti were moderate in all things, eating no unclean things taking only diluted wine, and mostly water, and rejecting sexual contact.

But their Way of Perfection was not understood by the Roman priests who, therefore, told these false stories; yet the common people of the villages, fields and mountains and markets knew the good life of the Perfecti, that these were those to whom they could turn for healing in sickness, comfort in adversity, a light in dark and troubled times and a Holy Peace at their passing.

For our philosophy was of Love: Divine Love of the Good God for the souls, his children and in return, of these children for the Good God.

And yet many men and women were overcome by the snares of Asmodeus and did not follow our path but fell by the wayside.

And these will now be reborn, yet again, to service in a new garment of flesh until they come at last to see the Truth of the Good God whose children they are. For the Good God wastes no seeds. And the seeds of our life are the creation of the Good God, so that righteousness must at last conquer vice and depravity.

Yet those who have the true knowledge do not follow the paths of depravity, eschewing vice and corruption and eat not animal's flesh, nor do they consort in sexual intercourse unless only when they are not yet Perfected and have not yet learned enough to know that this only makes more bodies for more souls to use who know not truth. And yet those who are perfected do not look down upon those who have not learned; nor do they judge them, for it is said that the Good God alone has the right of judgement of the children, the souls that are seeds of God.

And the Perfected souls will instruct, cure and care for all other souls who ask and truly beseech for learning; and they will go forth, two by two, travelling wherever need is great; and as they go, not only do they teach Truth but they also serve by healing and by helping in all wise (all ways) those whom they find in their pathway.

And by this service of love are they beloved of the people, who will hide and help the Perfecti when there is need.

And now in the world of men is great need of healing and helping and of Truth, more than ever in these times of the burning of our peoples' bodies. For man has outstretched himself and has challenged the laws of the universe and of the Good God, and in this there is no health, but only harm. And so now is the time for all Perfected souls to come to help and heal yet again, because man will always do ill if he be not taught better.

And now there are many souls living in fleshly bodies who are Perfected Ones but who have come again to teach, to help and to heal. And so God bless you and may the Light That Shines in darkness be upon you.'

Received Writings:

'Love is an un-broken circle unto like the golden ring with which we signify union, it has no end and no beginning.
Love is never wasted, because it is a sustained thought, and thoughts are living things, which take on an especial energy and are self-perpetuating

The Love which we send out into the Universe reaches not only the object of our affections, but all that it touches, enveloping all in its path, and touching, with its golden beams, things which we cannot even imagine.

Who knows what a loving thought may do, what good it can effect, things, people and conditions which we cannot conceive of, may be improved and enlightened by Love.

Never believe that love is lost for like Life, Love is eternal and it is purified as it grows and develops through time and space. Love is the fabric from which spirits, greater and more progressed than ourselves, fashion goodness and healing.

Loving thoughts are stronger than any other energy except for Life itself, and they work hand in hand with Life, enriching and beautifying the spirits who originate them and the spirits which are touched by them.

Physical death cannot dim Love for, like Life itself, Love transcends death.

Love journeys on, through Time and Space, rising ever higher through the spheres of eternity, delighting all those Ministers of Light who do the work of the Infinite Spirit.

Love is not, and cannot be, wasted or tarnished, and it flows from the same Source, whatever its object may be, and whatever way it presents itself.

The love of a mother for her child, a husband for his wife,

a wife for her husband or of friend for friend, is of the same stuff as the compassion shown by Healer to patient, by the Comforter to the afflicted.

The Source of Love is the Great Source of energy from which flows all that is human all that is experienced and also all that is loved.

Every human soul issues from that Source, as does Love itself, Life itself and every aspect of Service in every sphere of being.

The Source of all Life and Love is that Infinite Energy which we call God – the Everlasting Intelligence: Love itself.'

A Received Writing.

'We must love one another, since we are brothers and sisters in God, and God loves us.
It therefore becomes us to love as God loves.
We do not seek power, except the power of Love.
We seek to follow humbly in the steps of the Christ Spirit.
We must cherish, teach and heal, the souls and bodies of men and women, so that they, too, may know the love of God, and so are protected from the wiles of the god of this world, who would enslave them.
We know that soul is greater than the body, for the physical body is formed of coarse clay and dries out and dies, while the spirit transcends death, living forever in the light of God.
It is for this reason that we are not as the Romans would have us, slaves to the church, but rather living souls who rise to the values of the Good God from whom we learn humility, peace, and joy.
We do not praise the physical body but we recognize the soul embodied, and tend the soul so that it becomes loving and beautiful.
In time the soul will be at one with God by the example of the Christ Spirit and there is nothing that the established church can do to us that can change that.
We see that all mankind both male and female have souls and may be educated and may be kept pure by love and service, and by never cheating, by never swearing oaths, by working at trades honestly and by study of the life of the Christ Spirit. How much more joyful then shall we be when, as we live

spiritually, we live a life of Light, Love and wonder, rejoined with the Good God.
A draught of cool, pure water is our Faith in a dark world.'
From a conversation held between Llyn, Braida de Monserver, and Guilhabert de Castres on the 14th of October 2013.

Braida spoke first.

'You know, dear Friend, Consolamentum, and in fact all rituals are for the purpose of movement, and the words are to soothe the soul so that it may rise towards God; all rituals are for this purpose'

Braida's Song.
'We will make gardens
to please the souls of men.
and lakes, to nourish them;
we will paint pictures
for the eyes of men
to lavish beauty on them.
We will embroider cloths
to take the minds of women
to the deep-centred heart
of what we ever teach
and what we ever preach:
the Word of Light and Love.'

(Braida, a noblewoman and by then an elderly lady, was one of the 225 Cathars burned alive in 1244 in the massacre at Montsegur)

Then the Bishop spoke:

'So, you have driven around the hills, my son, and gone up the mountains – the Pic du Midi: well done, both of you! It is not the will of the Good God to suspend His servants above the ravine by a thread…….. but you have survived – rejoice! Regard your determination and also your total fright; there will be a time when this very thing will be that which is a perfect description for others to understand. When we are in the high mountains, we feel closer to God, because then we are closer to God; be aware that the Good God will never forsake you. Use every ounce of your experience, both good and bad, and make it work for the good.

You can turn all the bad experiences to good use.

You have been tried in the fire and found to be of gold.

We could not be more delighted with you.

You go home tomorrow, away from Occitania. This visit was planned by us to show you what forged you, what made you the man you were then, and to see the place where you were born and where you formed your being, in our times.

You have changed little by little, step by step.

You have moved closer to our souls' purpose, which is to come closer to the Good God.

> The eternal purpose is progress:All progress is brought about by knowledge, and by Love. All our incarnations are for the purposes of progress.

Love is necessary for it is so much needed in the world of flesh now.

All that really matters is Love!'

12 - Conclusion by Llyn

I have recently counted twenty three factual books about the Cathars, currently in print, both in English and in French – and this does not include the novels on offer.

There are two main streams of writing on this subject: the academic books, which are usually well researched and historically accurate, but dependant on the few surviving records from the period (mostly Inquisition documents), and the slightly more Gnostic/Theological books which compare and contrast other religious movements and belief systems with Catharism, speculating on the origins of all. There are also imaginative novels.

Dr. Arthur Guirdham's books on the Cathars stand alone in that his presentation of his, and others' experiences of spontaneous past-life memories and how they, over time, developed connections with him and with some of the people in his acquaintance.

Dr Guirdham wrote of his experiences with his associates, the verifications for which were confirmed through well respected academics of Cathar history.

He thoroughly researched the information given, in order to satisfy his own exacting standards as both a scientist and a doctor, and also in order to satisfy the potential critics amongst his readership.

He searched for the truth behind the experiences, and always strove to present them in the most honest and straightforward way.

Dr. Guirdham went to great lengths to protect his sources, the people whom he had met and connected with, all of whom shared memories of a previous, Cathar, lifetime.

In my opinion he is deserving of great respect, in presenting for publication subject matter which was potentially sensational and which may possibly have been regarded as inflammatory in some quarters: faith is a strange thing, and can, it would seem, be easily offended.

He further wrote of his experience of a group of souls who had re-incarnated again and again, and who had been able to remember and re-establish those old relationships, and to connect together, again.

The next big shift in awareness, for me, the culmination of these experiences, was when Audree showed me the first automatic writings from the Cathars in Spirit: they came thick and fast, and the authors identified themselves.

There were reams of it, and it was so eloquent, succinct and explanatory – it was as if they thought that we needed further guidance and instruction; they were, of course, establishing their credentials.

What struck me at the time was that it was so obvious that different writings were by different personalities, dare I say by different hands. We have come gradually, over the sixteen years, to trust them, and have found ourselves prepared to trust their guidance.

To my knowledge they have never misled us on any matter about which they have written or spoken.

We have elected to use pseudonyms, for ourselves and for our acquaintances, in order to protect peoples' careers, and our loved ones, and ourselves, from unwanted attention, having taken our cue from Dr. Guirdham's wisdom in this matter.

We have written rather less about talking directly to disembodied Cathar spirits, although that has happened, because we are, both as previously stated, working Mediums, and this type of ability tends to go with the territory, so we both take this rather for granted, and forget that that others may find this aspect of our work sensationalist, or even a little scary.

We find it perfectly normal: it goes with our skill-set.

With all these developments following from one to another in such quick succession, it has been an interesting exercise to write about, and a good discipline for us.

We have had to think very carefully about which was the clearest way in which to present the material.

Eventually, our mutual feeling was that all the material would have to be be presented as a series of our experiences, interlacing some of the automatic scripts, and some of the poems, and our personal reflections on them.. We thought it wise to present it more or less chronologically in order to make sense of the sixteen years which the material represents. At no point did we consider writing it as a novel, in some desperate attempt to get published.

The Cathars have themselves told us that their spiritual message remains as relevant to people today as it was to the people of the Languedoc (Occitania) over 800 years ago.

In their words 'The Inquisition could burn our bodies, but could not burn our souls. For look! We are still here!'

We offer the work for publication as our honest and loving dedication to the many thousands of Good Men and Good Women, and their believers, who faithfully served the Good God with their whole hearts and with their lives, and who glorified His name as they passed from that life into Martyrdom, at the hands of the 'Holy Office of the Inquisition' and the 'crusaders'.

May the Good God bless them always!

13 - Conclusion by Audree.

From the visits of our Cathar brothers and sisters and from the automatic scripts which they have sent via my 'automatic', or rather, sleeping, writing, and by using my voice while I have been 'asleep', we have had confirmed a great deal more that we can actually have found out about Cathar beliefs, and much more than we have found in such books as we have since read on the subject.

We have also had confirmation of daily lives, dress, how Cathars made a living and their relations with the communities in which they lived and worked.

That they were Healers who had a clear insight into the need for cleanliness – unusual in that time, has also been confirmed.

It has been such a great privilege to be able to meet with and know our Cathar friends,to work with them and for them and thus involved with bringing their ideals to life once more.

For this was not dust-dry research, this was contact with living entities who have distinct personalities and are warm, loving and humane.

We have further discovered that the Perfecti had mastered the esoteric art of withdrawing the spirit from the body at will.

This meant that they did not wait to suffer when 'burnt at the stake', but left the physical garment and went straight away to the spiritual realms – a great gift from the Good God whom they served.

An important aspect of their lives in those days was the joy and laughter which they enjoyed - people made their own pleasures and Perfecti joined in with them wherever it was not against their principles to do so, with singing, music, story-telling and even dancing – they were not enjoined to be unsociable, only not to sin!

It was always a pleasure to them to sit with friends under a sheltering vine, drinking the good wine of the country and eating the crusty, wholesome bread, with a few cherries or olives to help it down!

And of course it was from the Cathar respect for women that the idea of Courtly Love evolved. As did the tradition of the troubadours, whose songs of 'love' frequently had hidden meanings: they were often expositions of the Cathar beliefs were disguised as their love for an 'unattainable Lady': in reality 'she' was the Pistis Sophia, the Holy Wisdom: the Truth.

When all is said and done and written, it is all about Love.

Had the 'Cathars' not loved mankind they would not have bothered to contact us.Had we not loved both them and our fellow men and women we would not have bothered to write down what they have said or to type up what they have written – nor would we have bothered with this book.

All of it has been done for the Love of mankind and the Good God. We have learned to love the beautiful Languedoc, too, and we hope to return there and to learn more!

We have learned that we may choose to return to human life in a new body, should we feel it necessary for the progress of our souls.

Llyn recorded a conversation about the progress of souls, which she had with Guilhabert de Castres, through me, one evening during our stay in the Languedoc in 2013.

He explained that all rituals, rites and 'religious' forms of words were expressly to help souls make the next necessary step forward, whether this was from flesh life to spirit life, or from one stage of development to the next – like naming a child, marriage, or 'coming of age'.

The form of words of the Consolamentum was precisely to comfort the soul, reconcile it with itself, and so allow it to pass on to the next phase of its eternal life; the great goal being reunion with the Spirit of God. So it remains.

While most western religions seem to stop short at the side of the coffin, we, in company with Spiritualists and others, are now certain of the continuity of Life beyond physical death.

Catharism is a religion of Hope.

We say 'is' because we do not feel that we have outgrown the 'Cathar heresy' – we feel at one with it, just as did the Perfecti in the thirteenth century when, in company with other good souls they lived and worked for the Good God in that beautiful land, Occitania.

We have learned to look more deeply into matters, to try to see what else is there to be learned in life and to be open-minded about whatever we find.

The Cathars are all too frequently represented as severe and joyless – it has been confirmed to us that they were not, and are not, either severe or joyless. They were and still are, loving, forgiving, kindly and full of fun and laughter.

We have seen that there are many ways of approaching the Deity, and there is not only one, exclusive, way in which to pray and serve God.

Perhaps the most important and wonderful thing that we have learned to value above all else is that there is no death, and that we continue to exist beyond the demise of the physical body, as beings of spirit.

We think that the Cathar life of probity, sobriety, love for God and respect for mankind, and their simple joy, make a suitable spiritual pathway for those of the 21st Century who seek spiritual fulfilment and a way to love both God and their fellow men.

They have told us that the *only* way is Love.

Nothing really changes!

We intend to write about our own experiences both in the United Kingdom, and in the Languedoc in a future book.